THE PURPOSE OF YOUR LIFE
EXPERIENTIAL GUIDE

ALSO BY CAROL ADRIENNE

The Purpose of Your Life
The Numerology Kit
Your Child's Destiny: A Numerological Guide for Parents

COAUTHORED WITH JAMES REDFIELD

The Celestine Prophecy: An Experiential Guide
The Tenth Insight: Holding the Vision: An Experiential Guide

THE
PURPOSE
OF YOUR LIFE
EXPERIENTIAL
GUIDE

THE PROVEN PROGRAM TO HELP
YOU FIND YOUR REASON FOR BEING

Carol Adrienne

EAGLE BROOK
WILLIAM MORROW AND COMPANY, INC.
NEW YORK

Published by Eagle Brook
An Imprint of William Morrow and Company, Inc.
1350 Avenue of the Americas, New York, N.Y. 10019

It is the policy of William Morrow and Company, Inc., and its imprints
and affiliates, recognizing the importance of preserving what has been written,
to print the books we publish on acid-free paper,
and we exert our best efforts to that end.

Library of Congress Cataloging-in-Publication Data
Adrienne, Carol.
The purpose of your life experiential guide : the proven program
to help you find your reason for being / by Carol Adrienne. — 1st ed.
p.   cm.
"Eagle Brook."
A companion guide to The purpose of your life : finding your place in the world
using synchronicity, intuition, and uncommon sense.
ISBN 0-688-16714-4
1. Vocation. 2. Spiritual life. 3. Coincidence. 4. Intuition.
I. Title.
BL629.A369   1999
131—dc21   99–12818
CIP

Printed in the United States of America

First Edition

1 2 3 4 5 6 7 8 9 10

BOOK DESIGN BY OKSANA KUSHNIR

www.williammorrow.com

This book is dedicated to
all those who want to remember who they are
and who they've come to be.

ACKNOWLEDGMENTS

It is with great gratitude and humility that I want to acknowledge all the teachers of my life. My work could not exist without the network of spiritual and psychological influences I have been lucky enough to encounter, in books, in person, and in that invisible realm of inspiration. I am deeply grateful for all the people who have come forward to share their stories and journeys with me, and who have exemplified the value of an examined life. May I continue to meet you on the path.

On a personal level, I have to thank special friends who continue to be influential in helping me define and refine my thinking: Zenobia Barlow, Max Wellspring, Elizabeth Jenkins, Larry Leigon, Donna Hale, Penney Peirce, Nancy Rosanoff, Dr. Selma Lewis, Dianne Aigaki, Patricia Whitt, Georgia Rogers, and, of course, my daughter, Sigrid Emerson, with whom teaching this material has been a delight.

I especially want to thank my professional support team of outstanding women: my agent, Candice Fuhrman, for being the best, and for helping me to keep things simple; Linda Michaels, whose foreign rights agency has created wonderful adventures for me in other countries; my brilliant (yes, you are) editor, Joann Davis, for her exceptional support, unswerving vision, and eagle's eye on what really matters. I also want to thank Silvia Hines for her beyond-the-call-of-duty editing the complexities of this text; the publisher; and all the bookstores who take the book to the next step into the hands of the reading public.

We're all in this together.

CONTENTS

PART FIVE

BEING IT, DOING IT

PART SIX

MOVING FORWARD INTO THE TWENTY-FIRST CENTURY

For the unconscious always tries to produce an impossible situation in order to force the individual to bring out his very best. Otherwise one stops short of one's best, one is not complete, one does not realize oneself. What is needed is an impossible situation where one has to renounce one's own will and one's own wit and do nothing but wait and trust to the impersonal power of growth and development.

When you are up against a wall, be still and put down roots like a tree, until clarity comes from deeper sources to see over that wall.

—DR. CARL JUNG

Who Can This Book Help?

This book is for anyone who wants

- To be able to say, "I'm excited to wake up each morning and follow the path I know I'm supposed to be on."
- Techniques for staying focused and organized, yet flexible and open.
- To leave his or her job and move on to something better.
- To know what his or her passion is.
- To attract the right opportunities effortlessly.
- An alternative to the traditional "five-year-plan" approach to life.
- Security and freedom together.
- To do his own thing but doesn't have a clue how to start.
- To feel she is living the life she was born to live.
- To develop intuition in balance with logic.
- To learn to let life's "coincidences" open doors to opportunities she never dreamed were possible.
- To awaken to the contribution each of us can make in the coming transition into the new millennium.

The Purpose of the Workbook

This workbook is intended to help you feel that you are working in alignment with your life purpose. Each exercise or tip is made as simple as possible to help you

- Get organized
- Stay focused
- Handle fears around the unknown and changes
- Attract new opportunities
- Accomplish a change for the better for you and the world

Is It Better to Open the Book at Random or Read It Chapter by Chapter?

Your life purpose shows up everywhere and is part of every interaction and activity. Therefore, you need not start at the beginning of this book and work straight through to completion. Some people like to open the book and start anywhere, trusting that whatever exercise they find at that moment will be appropriate. Other people like to do one or two exercises, stop for a month or longer, and then do a new one. Still others prefer to start at Chapter 1 and work on the material weekly or daily in a step-by-step method. There is no right way. The most important point is to feel enjoyment as you read or write or work on the exercises.

Make Your Own Oracle and Reminder Cards (TIP CARDS)

In Chapter 8 I give instructions for making your own oracles by putting words and images on index cards. Whenever you have a life question, you can draw one to seven cards to stimulate your intuitive knowing.

One some pages I have written the words TIP CARDS, with a simple direction to write an insight on an index card to keep handy for times when you need a little inspiration! You might want to keep index cards handy as you read this book, to jot down notes as you go. A stack of notes is often more useful for referring to on the spur of the moment than notes written down on pages in a notebook.

Draw a Profile of Yourself and Discover Your Life Purpose

The Profile of Purpose sheets at the back of this book are a unique feature, a summary of some of the major exercises you will do in the workbook. As you complete an exercise, you will be asked to transfer part of your insights or answers from that exercise to the corresponding Profile sheet. Therefore, even if you do the exercises in a random way, you will always have a record of what you have learned. Once you have completed the profile sheets, you will have a portrait of who you are and what you are looking for in life!

Use This Book to Increase Consciousness in Handling Special Projects

Even though you bought this book to help you tune into your life purpose and find your place in the world, you can also use this book whenever you have special situations that you want to face more consciously. For example, when starting a project, turn to Chapter 1, Getting Started. The ideas listed there may help you get centered as you go forward on the project.

PART ONE

STARTING
WHERE YOU ARE

CHAPTER 1

Getting Started

Masked by the snowflakes,
The colour of your petals
May well be hidden:
Yet still put forth your scent
That people may know your flower.

—ONO TAKAMURA[1]

Each of us dreams of reaching a point at which we finally "have it all together." Often we assume that today "doesn't really count." It's just another day. But this day is an entire and beautiful gift, full of physical sensations, a range of emotional responses, and information about who we are and why we are here—if we choose to become conscious of what this day brings. Each day has its own purpose and fits into the great plan of our life. This very moment carries traces of our life purpose in places where we focus our attention, in words or ideas that bring a tingle of excitement and hope in our heart.

Your life purpose was chosen before birth. This inborn organizing force silently attracts people and information directly related to what you need to know in order to make immediate choices. Someone may recommend a book, a teacher, a job opportunity, or a blind date. You may take a wrong turn and wind up at the right place. This workbook is designed to help you awaken to the natural guidance of your intuition and to stay in the flow of effortless synchronicity. Let's start by getting into the feel of what you want.

WHAT ARE YOU LOOKING FOR?

Close your eyes and remember a time when you felt fully alive and so engrossed in something that you lost track of the time. Try to reexperience this scene of success and self-confidence. How did you feel? How would you describe your feelings at the peak of being yourself, on your path, on purpose?

Others describe their feelings of being on purpose as follows:

- Work feels effortless.
- Everything flows.
- I can handle anything.
- I'm in tune.
- Money flows in.
- Synchronicities abound.
- I'm totally absorbed.
- I'm doing service.
- It's fun.
- I feel resourceful.
- I feel a passion for the work.
- I feel motivated.
- I have more courage.
- I'm energized.
- I'm excited.

These states of being are all proof that you have already been able to connect to something you value, something that is part of your purpose. If you can truthfully say that you have never had any of these feelings, perhaps you can close your eyes and bring those desired states fully into your being by playfully pretending to feel the joy of being on track. When you experience any of these feeling states, you are on track and on purpose.

To help you describe and define this deep inner yearning to find your place in the world, to live your purpose, take a moment to answer the following questions as best you can. Don't struggle or strain to come up with any fancy words. Just write out what is in your heart at this moment.

1. What is so important to you that you bought this book to work on finding your life purpose?_____

_____

_____

2. What are you looking for?_____

_____

_____

3. What do you want?_____

_____

4. What would make you happy?_____

_____

5. What stops you from having it?_____

_____

6. How do you want to feel?_____

_____

7. What have you been passionate about in the past?_____

_____

8. If you could have anything you want, what would that be?_____

_____

9. What aspects of your life or career are you truly committed to?

_____

10. What would make a difference in the quality of your life?_____

_____

11. If you had the thing that would make a difference in the quality of your life, what would that give you?_____

_____

12. What would you like to change in the world?_____

_____

13. What would it take for you to be living in total integrity?_____

_____

_____

✔ Transfer your answers to questions 1, 2, 4, 6, 11, and 13 to the profile sheet, pages 223–224.

POINTS TO REMEMBER WHEN GETTING STARTED

✔ **Stay open and express gratitude for what you already have.**
  • Today is a new day. No matter what has gone before, today is a completely new gift from God for you to enjoy.
  • Anything might happen today. Anything is possible.
  • You are always at the *beginning*.
  • You always have options.

✔ **If you don't know where to start**
  • Start anywhere. Start wherever you are. Take small steps in the direction you want to go. When you procrastinate, *especially when you know what the next step should be*, you drain your energy. Starting anywhere means you can begin to be on purpose by cleaning out your garage, taking your child to the park, or inviting friends over to brainstorm a community project. When you put your heart and mind together to do the best you can in any situation, you are working from a sense of purpose, which will lead you to being more fully expressed.
  • Take one small step. Then take another.
  • Watch to see what happens next. Do you get a go or a no from life?
  • Do any coincidences suggest new options?
  • What does your intuition or gut suggest?
  • Remember that there is a reason for everything.
  • Stay in the moment. The present moment contains clues, messages, and opportunities.
  • Ask yourself: What is my conscious excuse or reason for stalling? What do I gain from stalling? What is the fear underneath the excuse or reason?

TIP CARDS: On individual index cards, write the tips that give you the most energy.

THE OPRAH STORY

I tell this story because it illustrates several points about the process of unfolding life purpose. Perhaps the main point of this story is that when we want to increase our prosperity and success, we literally have to "raise the ceiling" on our beliefs about ourselves. Raising the ceiling opens the space for the next piece of abundance to flow in.

During the weeks before *The Purpose of Your Life* came out, I was preparing to promote the book with my publisher's help. I was concerned about how to present the book in appropriate "sound bytes"— those short, high-impact messages necessary for radio and TV programs. Even though the book was not yet available, I needed to brainstorm with someone who knew the ropes, and my intuition suggested my friend Larry Leigon. Larry is a business consultant who, at one time, traveled widely promoting Ariel, a nonalcoholic winery he cofounded.

Settling down in my office with him on a Friday morning, I was geared up to attack my book, chapter by chapter, in a linear way, looking for the most important points. Instead, Larry asked me, "What interested you this morning?" Anticipating that I somehow was going to have to struggle to find and prioritize ideas, and labor to find the right words, I found Larry's question disarmingly easy to answer. Surprised, I felt a relaxation in my body. All I had to do was think back to earlier in the morning when I read the newspaper. "I was interested in a story about the mayor of Naples who is cleaning up crime in his city," I told Larry. "Why?" he asked. I told him I was interested in people who make a difference in the world. Also, I was getting ready to go to Italy to teach workshops, and this was a good story of someone in that country manifesting his life purpose.

"What did you do with the article?" he continued to probe. I said I had cut it out, underlined some ideas, made some notes, and filed it. "Of course, you did. You're a writer," he said, laughing. "Something about that article was important to your life purpose." "Wow," I exclaimed. "That's so interesting, Larry! *You* should be teaching this material. How did you come up with that?" "Easy," he replied. "I got it out of your book [*The Purpose of Your Life*]." He was mirroring back to me the very point I make to others. In my experience, anything that catches our interest is part of our life purpose, or we wouldn't be paying attention to it. Shaking my head with good-humored chagrin, I continued to answer his questions about what interests me and why. (Synchronicistically, I met the mayor of Palermo, Leoluca Orlando, another Sicilian crime-fighting public figure, when we both appeared on the Michael Jackson show on KRLA exactly one year later to the day.)

By getting clear about what I do in my writing, workshops, and numerology consultations, I formulated a purpose statement for my work. It seems that what I tend to do, time after time, is help people pay attention to what they normally overlook.

"So how many people would you like to do that for?" he asked. I thought back to when I began my practice with small classes of six or seven people. In the past few years, I have traveled extensively and figured that maybe the largest audience I had had so far was about fifteen hundred. "How would you like to talk to a hundred thousand?" he asked. Whoa. One hundred thousand? Larry described my reaction as "backing away" from that idea, rather than moving toward it. I realized I was intimidated by the idea of such a large crowd. Why was I so intimidated?

As I examined my feelings, I realized that I was suffering from a faulty conception of what would be required of me at this theoretical event. If all I had to do was "do my life purpose," which is to help people pay attention to what they would normally overlook, then it wouldn't matter who was in front of me. What had momentarily stopped me from moving toward the idea of a large crowd was not understanding my part in the overall structure. I did not have to park all the cars. I did not have to sell the tickets. I did not have to cater the event. Others would find an outlet for their interests and abilities in doing these other activities. All *I* had to do was stand on the stage and help people pay attention to what they would normally overlook. That's my part. I was energized by our work together, and Larry left after a quick lunch.

About four hours later, the producer from *Oprah* called and formally invited me to appear on the show they were doing about synchronicity. You can't tell me that those two events—imagining myself at ease speaking to thousands of people and receiving a call from the most-watched television show in America—were not related. I had raised the ceiling on my identity as a speaker.

Let's review some of the lessons and points from the story.

- *My intuition prompted me to seek help.* Ostensibly, my intuition was telling me that my next step was to find help with promotional issues. However, there was an issue that was deeper than that simple promotion, and it lay in my unconscious, asking to come to the light of awareness.

- Again, *following intuition and uncommon sense*, rather than logically going to the phone book, I selected someone who was familiar with my book and experiences but was not a professional media coach. The commonsense answer would have been to hire a public relations person (which I also did later, by the way).

- *Defining my own purpose helped me see exactly what I do—and what I don't do.* This clarification brought up deep, related issues about my self-concept, issues that needed to be addressed so that a larger flow could happen. The specific concern about sound bytes, as is so often the case with our fears, was not the important issue.

- *I saw the ceiling I had put on myself.* This realization allowed me to see that my fear of the event stemmed from misidentifying the true nature of my task. Realizing that all I had to do was what I love to do and am good at doing took most of the fear away. I didn't "conquer the fear;" I looked at it and saw that I was fearful of things that weren't mine to deal with.

- Identifying my purpose, being willing to show up and do my purpose, and not getting sidetracked into irrelevant fears seemed to open my energy field and attract in the special opportunity of being on a stage reaching far more than a hundred thousand people.

You will be able to work with some of these principles in the next chapter. Before that, however, read about how Christina (Sunni) Taliaferro, founder and visionary of Wings of Solimar, an angel gallery, made the transition from being a successful but burnt-out marketing executive in the music business to becoming owner of a spiritual center in Lafayette, California.

> "At this moment, you are in a stage of your developing purpose, and you are not off track, no matter how blocked you currently feel. Your calling has already made itself known through what motivates you (past and present), what attracts you, what you resist, and what frustrates you. Your calling may have made a brief appearance between the ages of three and eight, or revealed itself in adolescence through a sudden interest. Your calling can also be glimpsed in what you admire in others. It can be seen in those abilities you have that you don't even think are special."
>
> —The Purpose of Your Life[2]

SUNNI'S STORY

"I had been working in the glitzy world of the music business but was completely exhausted and unsatisfied. I didn't know what to do. In 1993 I read *The Celestine Prophecy* [by James Redfield] five times and *The Celestine Prophecy: An Experiential Guide* [by Redfield and Adrienne] twice. I decided I wanted to go within. I reviewed the milestones of my life, and wrote it all out. I saw that I needed to learn compassion, and I saw that I had not forgiven myself or the people who have hurt me. It felt like my soul was broken. I was looking for a place to learn humility. That turned out to be as a bagger at Lucky's [supermarket]. You don't get much more subservient than bagging people's groceries!

"I heard Deepak Chopra say that we must walk through life without judgment, and I wanted to be able to do that. I would stand at the end of the checkout line and greet everyone with a smile. I would silently say to them, 'The God Light in me salutes the God Light in you.' Many people would be puzzled and ask me, 'Why are you a bagger?' I said, 'I'm in transition; I'm learning,' but I didn't let anyone know that I was doing this job as a spiritual practice.

"I would push grocery carts in the rain, and some people wouldn't even say good-bye to me. Even so, I'd still go up to their window and say, 'Have a nice day.' I would still send them love; it occurred to me that maybe I was the only person in their life who would give them positive energy that day. For every cart I pushed, I would say to myself, 'This is a test of my will to surrender and to grow as a spirit.'

"I learned that the glass ceiling can be pushed through when you are working from the spiritual level. Normally, grocery stores are extremely hierarchical and seniority is everything. Within six months I was promoted to bookkeeper, which sent shock waves through the store, since I was such a new kid on the block. But the hostility from older employees just died away in the face of my attitude. I still didn't say anything about my spiritual practice or that I had already had a career in the music business. I learned so much at Lucky's! I can't even tell you.

"Believing in yourself can change almost any circumstance. Things unbeknownst to you can change your life. I transformed my life literally by giving my love every day and walking without judgment."

Sunni continued at Lucky's for a year, after which she got the clear message that it was time to quit. Furthermore, on December 13 she had an amazing experience she readily describes as a visitation from two angels. These beings communicated to her that her task was to start an angel store. The next morning Sunni's mother called her at 6:30 A.M. She had had a dream that Sunni was going to start a new business, and that she, her mother, was supposed to help her.

"I knew then that I was supposed to bring the intangible into the tangible world, but that's all the specific direction I received. Then the coincidences started to happen. Helpful people started to show up. I moved with warp speed. My intuition would say, 'Turn left,' and I would, or 'Go to this meeting,' and I would meet the next crucial person. Living like this became my way of being. It was very clear. I knew I had to walk a living prayer. I literally started each day by asking, 'What do I do first?' I'd brush my teeth and then ask, 'What next?'

"I was still bulimic at this time, and I began to listen to my inner voice. I learned to distinguish the rabid voice that said, 'Eat, eat, eat,' which also made me eat faster. By being able to feel the urgency of that voice, I could then choose to eat slower. The voice that told me I was fat didn't match the slower pace of eating. I started hearing another voice that said, 'It's okay to nourish your body.' Gradually, learning to listen to the intuitive voice brought me back to health.

"During this two-year period of transformation, everything came about from paying attention to and following my intuition. Everything flowed. For example, I needed a corporate office for the gallery, and I really wanted it to be next door, but there was nothing available. I prayed for a space. A couple of days later, there was a For Lease sign on the building next door. The travel agent who had been there for seven years had decided to close her business. I couldn't believe my eyes! Even so, I thought, 'Oh, I'll never be able to get it.' But we did. Guess what? The suite address was A—for angel!

"I've learned that when I start forgetting about the invisible world, I just remember I am only human and be gentle with myself. When I fall down, all I have to do is get back up."

I asked Sunni to describe some specifics about her journey to fulfill her life purpose:

CA: Do you think you could have done the "spiritual humility" practice you did at Lucky's if you had stayed at the job you had in the music business?

ST: No. My music-promoting job represented the status quo. Working in that business forced me to define myself by external image and external success. Everything there is based on "How do you look? Who do you know?" I didn't feel I could be me there. In fact I was asked to tone down my enthusiasm because it caused jealousy among my colleagues. I had to do whatever I could to get a record played, and every interaction was competitive. It felt like everyone was stealing energy from each other.

You're told, "Don't process your feelings here. Don't take no for an answer, and keep a stiff upper lip. Wear the shortest skirts possible and be able to dance on tables." You don't really care about others. You're always competing. I am open by nature, but when you're trying to adapt to an environment that is foreign to your nature, you feel conflict. I was walking around in fear of losing my job. This also caused me to continue my bulimia. Too much depended on working for the artists and the bottom line. I never found the time to do my spiritual work. But working in the subservient position of being a bagger at Lucky's, I had a whole lot of time to think! It wasn't mentally demanding.

CA: Can you tell me how you feel different now?

ST: In my marketing jobs I was in a constant state of envy and jealousy, both feeling it and receiving it. I felt my spirit was clipped. Now I have more female friends. I feel it's okay to be who I am. I remind myself now that what other people think of me is none of my business. When you worry about what people think about you, you allow them to take your energy. I've let go of a lot of people who drain me. Going within is where I go now for answers.

Before, I believed I was important if I had the right man, the right home, the car, all the trips, and the accolades for being on top. The truth was I was down, depressed, and unsatisfied. I traveled. I met the celebrities. I had everything that people want, but I was lonely, bulimic, and suicidal.

> "Pathways and habits develop. . . . Who we are becomes an expression of who we decided to be. . . . The world asks that we focus less on how we can coerce something to make it conform to our designs and focus more on how we can engage with one another, how we can enter into the experience and then notice what comes forth. It asks that we participate more than plan."
>
> —Wheatley and Kellner Rogers[3]

CA: What did you do first?

ST: Well, after I read *The Celestine Prophecy* and the *Experiential Guide* books, I had a completely new way to look at how I wanted to live and what could be possible. I was so excited. I kept looking at what I really wanted in life, and I knew something had to go. I left my fiancé. I sold my clothes. I gave everything away. I had nothing. I'm not saying you have to be broke to be spiritual. Not at all. But my focus had been so strongly on money and my career, I felt I had to start from scratch. I had become dependent on my man and my job to be the judge and jury of my life. And that failed me.

CA: So, in a nutshell, what can you say worked for you?

ST: First, I stopped looking to the external world for my abundance. Second, I had a strong desire to change my thinking and belief about who I thought I was. Third, I had to accept things that I could not change. I thought, "The world is what it is, but who am I in it?" Fourth, I took action to change the way I was living. I left my job, my relationship, and the town where I had been living. I went back to nature to get quiet because I was living in static. Then the knowing started to come. When you let go of distractions (friends, parties, negative relationships), you start to sit in silence. For me, the quickest way to spirituality is to get quiet.

I would watch plants for two hours at a time. At first I didn't see anything, but gradually I could see the energy around them. Then I began to practice seeing my own energy field. Seeing the energy in plants and myself allowed me, for the first time in my life, to have the courage to believe in myself. It propelled me to continue. I became more open, even though I didn't sit down and say I want to be more open. I would sit in a café and read my spiritual books and practice sending out positive energy. I'd smile at strangers and say hello. I started to make new friends because of it. Synchronicities started to happen constantly. Now I live this way all the time.

Insights from Sunni's Story

Underline any passage in the story that touched you. In what way could you benefit from this story? Is there any action that suggests itself to you? If so, write your thought here:

_____

_____

_____

_____

SIX PRINCIPLES FOR ALIGNING WITH YOUR LIFE MISSION

1. *Act on Passion.* Act when you feel a "go" type of energy. Do more of what you like to do. Your passion shows up in the things with which you lose track of time.
2. *Be discerning.* Stop doing things where you are just putting in time. Pay attention to shifts in your body signals. Question your motives when making choices.
3. *Listen.* Follow through on persistent intuitive messages. Listen for the opportunity that someone may suggest.
4. *Commit.* Do whatever it takes to put you in motion toward what your intuition is telling you to do.
5. *Stay open.* You never know. Anything is possible.
6. *Trust.* Trust the process you are in. There are no accidents.

Adapted from The Purpose of Your Life[4]

DAILY CHECK-IN

Become conscious of how you are participating in your daily life. For example, ask yourself these questions:

- *Looking back on today, do I have any unfinished business with anyone?*

- *Is there any top priority issue to resolve?*

- *If so, what am I willing to do about it? When?*

- *What is my intuition telling me to do or pay attention to?*

TIP CARD: Write any insights you want to remember on separate index cards to keep handy.

CHAPTER 2

Initiation

During the course of our lives we've all been touched by sublime influences that leave indelible marks on our sensitivities: encounters with great art, poetry, music; certain experiences in nature; times in love; even moments of danger when we feel intensely and heartbreakingly alive. At such moments we realize that our customary life is by no means our real life, and that there is a quickened, magical state of being hovering just above the rim of our everyday awareness.

—Harry R. Moody[1]

In virtually every traditional culture, ceremonies, rituals, and initiations mark important transitions. Perhaps it is time for you to cross over into a "new land." Depending on your background, the idea of an initiation may seem a bit intimidating. However, a ritual is essentially about bringing a certain mindfulness to whatever you are doing. For example, we have common rituals, such as washing our hands before partaking of a meal or saying grace at the table. We might have personal rituals of setting up our desk for work in a certain way or setting our tables with special dishes or utensils for a festive meal. If you have decided to undertake your own initiation, plan to set aside a day, a weekend, or even longer. This will give you a special time to review your life, get in touch with where you are now, and experience the beauty of each moment.

Your day of contemplation should be a time of cleansing, simplifying, releasing, and quietening so that you can meet yourself, glean some insights about where you have been in life, and hear the still, small voice of your intuition taking you into the next adventure.

Create your own ritual. Below are a few ideas to get you started, but don't try to do all of them in one day! Select the ideas that seem most interesting or fun to you. Feel free to add any inspiring ideas that occur to you. At the end of this section, you can find out the symbolic meaning of the date that you chose. You may also want to use some of these ideas for special occasions such as New Year's Day or your birthday.

FIVE LEVELS OF MINDFULNESS

Physical Mindfulness

✔ **Select as many of these as you like:**
  • Get as much sleep as you can the night before.
  • Awaken on your own time.
  • Take time to bathe with a new bar of soap. Wash your hand, and thank it for all the things it does for you. Continue with all parts of your body.
  • Put on freshly laundered clothes that are comfortable and make you feel good.
  • Avoid watching any TV or reading any newspapers or news-magazines during your specified initiation period (all day, all weekend, or whatever period of time you have chosen).
  • Eat simply, only and whenever you are hungry.
  • Sit in silence twice during the day for at least fifteen minutes each time. While sitting, let your thoughts drift away without trying to figure out anything.
  • Get extra sleep during the day.
  • If you're really brave, keep the ringer on your phone off all day.
  • Walk around your house or your room and notice what kind of person or persons live there (you, your family).
  • With no sense of doing anything in particular, no urgency, just notice your surroundings. If any organizing or readjustments need to be made, do them with as full attention as you can give. Move slowly and leisurely. If nothing seems all that important to do, sit quietly until you receive inspiration concerning what to do next. Be willing to let the day unfold.

Emotional Mindfulness

✔ **Select one or two of the following to do:**
- Walk somewhere with no purpose, preferably in an unfamiliar area. Be attentive to small details, smells, noises, people, flowers, the earth, trees, and sun.
- Write a letter of forgiveness to someone.
- Write two thank you notes to people you love, just for being in your life.
- Sit quietly and imagine that with each breath, your heart is opening wide to send and receive love.
- Perform at least one anonymous act of kindness during the day.
- Speak to someone you don't know.
- Think of someone you want to know better and plan to invite him or her over for a cup of tea next week.
- Put a flower on your table.

Mental Mindfulness

✔ **Select one or two of the following to do:**
- Write down the details of a moment in the day as if it were a dream.
- Notice what things attract your attention. Jot down a note about that on the Initiation section of your profile sheet, page 225.
- Choose one moment during the day and describe this scene in four lines, as though writing Japanese haiku poetry. Notice how easily you can write poetry! In a week or so, reread your poem, and notice that whatever you chose to write about is somehow related to your current life purpose.
- Find one book you already have and open to a random page. Write down any insight that speaks to you at this moment.
- Remember to say, in the morning, "Today I want to meet good people."
- As you walk, think to yourself, "Energy in. Problems out."

Financial Mindfulness
- Sit quietly and feel gratitude for all that you possess.
- Buy nothing all day except food or meals.

- Give away three things you no longer use.
- Give away 10 percent of any money you have in your wallet to the first person who seems to need it more than you do.

Spiritual Mindfulness

✔ **Try to find an activity that refreshes and inspires you, such as the following:**
   - Clear one small space on a bureau or table and put objects there that are meaningful to you: a cloth, photos, fresh flowers, special keepsakes, a candle. It's helpful to have a visual reminder of your spiritual connections.
   - Take a few moments to relax with eyes closed. Take a few soft, deep inhalations. Imagine a door in front of you. Ask for a spiritual guide to come to the door, and gently ask the door to open. Whom do you see? Ask your guide his or her name, and offer any question to the guide that is in your heart today. You may want to ask your guide to give you a symbol that will represent his or her presence in your life.
   - Do *nothing* for two hours. You might try a walking meditation by keeping your attention on each foot rising and falling. You might want to lie on the grass and watch the clouds or lie on your bed and listen to the sounds around your room. Notice how heavy your body is as it sinks into the bed or floor. It's okay to fall asleep.
   - Prepare for bed by taking a walk under the stars, sitting in your backyard under the sky, staring into a fire in the fireplace, reading an inspirational book, or meditating. Go to bed with a clear and peaceful sense that all your needs are being met.
   - Give thanks for all the abundance you experienced today. Send loving, positive thoughts to all those who met you, all those who are important to you, and all those you will meet in the future.
   - If you wish to find the resolution to a question, put a notebook and pencil next to your bed. Then, when you are ready to go to sleep, lie in bed with your legs straight, ankles crossed, and hands forming a triangle over your abdomen. Close your eyes and repeat one simple question three times. Pray to receive a clear message during your dream time. You may do this for three nights in a row. If you still receive no answer, then release the question until a later time.

CALCULATING THE NUMEROLOGICAL PERSONAL DAY FOR YOUR INITIATION

Choose a date to begin your initiation—perhaps a Saturday or Sunday, a vacation day, or any other free day when you will set aside other concerns, errands, or obligations. For example, one of our students, Carla, chose November 13, 1999.

Step 1. Add together all the numbers in the current year to find the Universal Year Number. For example, if you are doing your initiation during the year 1999, add $1 + 9 + 9 + 9 = 28$ $(2 + 8 = 10)$ $1 + 0 = 1$. The Universal Year Number for 1999 is therefore 1.

Step 2. *Add the month and day of your birthday to the Universal Year Number to find your Personal Year Number.* For example, Carla's birthday is October 23. Since October is the tenth month, she writes

October   23   1999
$1 + 0$ $+$ $2 + 3$ $+$ $1 =$ 7

Carla's Personal Year Number is 7.

Step 3. Add the month and day of your initiation to your Personal Year Number to find the symbolic meaning of your Personal Initiation Day. Carla wrote the date she chose, November 13, like this:

November   13   Personal Year 7
$1 + 1$ $+$ $1 + 3$ $+$ $7 =$ $13 = (1 + 3) = 4$

Carla's Personal Day Number on November 13, 1999, is 4.

MEANING OF THE PERSONAL DAY NUMBER AS AN INITIATION

Each day in the cycle from one to nine has its own special spiritual significance. All the numbers are positive and encouraging, but each one speaks to a different focus or energy pattern. Below is a brief interpretation of each personal day.

1   A day of new beginnings, particularly fosters self-confidence, creative and innovative ideas, integrity, inspired communication, strength, courage, and risk taking.

2   A day of deep intuitive connection, favors art, friendship, patience, stillness, resolution of conflict, attention to details, ability to create balance and beauty.

3   A day of joy, fosters optimism, good luck, friendship, serendipity, creativity, music, dancing, communication, abundance, and playfulness.

4   A day of deep commitment, favors resolution of outstanding problems, a feeling of power and competency, long-term planning, calmness, and practical creativity.

5   A day of adventure, fosters risk-taking and curiosity, openness to exploring, being in the moment, feeling vitally alive and ready for anything, quick solutions, and physical power.

6   A day of teaching and learning, favors being in the comfort of home, cozy, casual, resolution of family issues, calmness, music, art, and a feeling of prosperity.

7   A day of quiet reflection, requires solitude, meditation, journal writing, healing the body with silence and pure actions; favors being in nature, doing nothing, getting away.

8   A day of inner resolution and problem solving, fosters objectivity about plans, a feeling of great power, looking forward to the future and getting projects done.

9   A day of wholeness and unconditional love, fosters philosophical overview, opening of the heart, release of old pain, sense of completion and fulfillment, expansion and tolerance.

If the date you picked happens to add up to any of these compound (two-digit) numbers, then read the following descriptions as well as the description for the reduced total above (e.g., if your day adds up to 13, read 13 below and 4 above).

11   A day of high inspiration and intuitive connection. Very appropriate for higher understanding and opening new channels of awareness. Emotional sensitivity.

13   A day of rebirth and giving back. Favors a look at how we have chosen our path and agreed to work with certain important people in our life. Reliving painful memories.

14   A day of freedom from the shackles of addiction, fear, or guilt. May unlock a secret, but hard to stay quiet for meditation. May signal the advent of major change. Restlessness.

16 A day of catalyzing action to heal a chaotic or frozen situation. Thoughts of old loves, past suffering. Deeply spiritual and unusual experiences. Breakthroughs.

19 A day of intense personal scrutiny. Need for making more conscious choices, especially if one is in a leadership position; fosters strength of conviction, courage, and decisiveness.

22 A day of great insight and spiritual deepening toward being able to implement cherished goals. Be sure to write down all intuitive messages. Powerful and practical.

33 A day flooded with love of others and the desire to ease suffering. Be careful not to make promises that you can't keep! May help resolve very deep, old family issues.

✔ End your period of initiation by writing down five things you are willing to do for yourself and others, as well as something you would like support for from the universe. Record the significance of your personal day of initiation on page 225 of your profile sheet.

CHAPTER 3

The Bottom Lines of My Life Purpose— What Feels Most Important to Me

What is this thrall for houses? I come from a long line of women who open their handbags and take out swatches of upholstery material, colored squares of bathroom tile, seven shades of yellow paint samples, and strips of flowered wallpaper. We love the concept of four walls. "What is her house like?" my sister asks, and we both know she means what is she like.

—FRANCES MAYES[1]

The term *bottom line* is frequently used in our reductionist, results-oriented Western business culture to mean the essentials: "Cut the details. Give it to me straight. What's the profit (or loss) at the end of the deal?"

I use the term *bottom line* here to get you started looking at *exactly* what you most value and must have in your life. Ask yourself if your first thought is one of these: *I have to have my morning coffee!" I must have good friends in my life. I must have freedom. I have to work for myself. I need to feel I'm making a difference in someone's life. I have to live near nature; that's nonnegotiable.* As we begin to focus more consciously on what our needs and interests are, we further activate the law of attraction. Remember, what you focus on expands. Keep your focus on that for which you are grateful and that which you want to attract. Let the irritations drop away from focus.

In this chapter you can help define your bottom line by completing seven exercises and distilling your results in your Profile of Purpose at the back of the book. The exercises are:

- Drawing My Current Life Matrix
- The Wheel of Life Inventory
- Recognizing My Top Needs
- Recognizing My Primary Type
- What's My Line
- Which of Nine Career Paths Am I Following?
- What I Love to Do

The following is an easy and enjoyable exercise (you'll need at least thirty minutes to an hour) to help you define what you are currently about and where you'd like to go. The beauty of this exercise is fourfold: (1) It shows you how many wonderful things you have already created or been given by life. Therefore, you may find that you are not as far from your goal as you thought. (2) Acknowledging your actual abundance and success builds trust and confidence in yourself. (3) Using symbols to represent your life matrix stimulates powerful, magnetic unconscious forces. (4) Delineating your life matrix helps clarify the kind of overall path you are on. Therefore, when you look at what you have drawn on your page, ask yourself, "What kind of purpose does this person (you) seem to be fulfilling?"

DRAWING MY CURRENT LIFE MATRIX

What you need: white paper, pen or pencil (optional, colored pencils or crayons), a quiet place where you won't be bothered for about thirty minutes.

- *What I love about my life right now.* In the center of your page, using simple little symbols and stick figures, draw in everything you love in your life right now—everything that is nonnegotiable, everything that you cannot live without. These are people, places, and things that you *already have.* Draw everything in your life that you value, such as your children, family, friends, house, car, computer, colleagues, running shoes, church, books, trees (include intangibles such as, love, health, freedom, security, and education). It's important to draw them instead of using words.
- *What I want to attract.* In the upper right corner, draw symbols of specific things or people you would like to have in your life—what

> "I believe that what happened was that I had turned a corner about seeing who I was and wanting the company to fit for me—not trying to be who they wanted me to be at all costs."
> —Stefeni McKinzie,
> in *The Purpose of Your Life*[2]

you want to attract. Enclose these symbols with a large heart (so you can pump lifeblood into them).

• *What I want to release*. In the lower left corner, draw symbols to represent what you want to release, complete, and get rid of. Enclose these symbols inside a pair of big wings (so they can fly away).

• *My values*. Put value words under the depictions of the people, places, and things you love that you drew in the center of your page. If you have drawn a house, don't write *house*, but instead write down what the house gives you of value, for example, "a warm cozy retreat from the world" or "a comfortable place to work, live, and entertain friends and a good investment." If you drew a picture of your computer, ask yourself what value your computer provides for you; for example, "link to the outside world," "educational information," or "workstation to create my livelihood without commuting." If you drew a picture of your car, of what value is your car to you? Mobility? A statement of personal expression? Ability to get to your job and provide security for yourself? Freedom to get to the mountains for skiing? Ability to be responsible and take your kids to school?

• On the profile sheet in the back of your workbook, pages 225–226, write the value words for what you have in your life right now, what you want to attract, and what you want to release.

THE INVENTORY OF LIFE SATISFACTION

Sometimes when the zest has gone out of life, we tend to think *everything* is black and bleak. However, by taking a good look at each of the aspects of our life, we may be surprised to see that most of it is pretty good. Our dissatisfaction may lie in a specific area, which can be changed for the better by bringing more attention and intention to it. By filling out the following Inventory of Life Satisfaction, you will have an opportunity to assess each area of your life, and see what specific affirmations you can make to begin to enhance that part of your life.

The first step is to assign a number from one to ten (ten being complete or almost complete satisfaction) to each segment of your life's "pie." After reviewing the general balance of satisfaction, you might want to write your own affirmation of *how you'd like to feel* in each area in the future. For example, if you rate the money segment of your life at only a 2 or 3 level, you might write an affirmation such as, "Money flows in from a surprising number of sources" or some other version of this idea—based on wording that gives you an exciting lift of energy when you think about it. After bringing attention to the area, begin to notice any new information you receive or any people whom you meet who may have exactly what you need to increase the joy in your life. Some people also color in the segments with crayons. You can keep the Wheel in a visible place for a few days, but then put it away with full trust that the satisfaction you want is already on the way.

RECOGNIZING MY TOP NEEDS

What motivates you? Really. According to a particularly clear esoteric teaching explored by Jose Stevens, Ph.D., author of *The Michael Handbook*, there are nine basic needs that motivate us, listed below. Perhaps these needs provide another way to look at what we call *life purpose*. If so, these basic, inborn drives would be so important that we could not help but seek their fulfillment.

✔ **Find your top three needs.** Take a look at the following choices, and select three that most seem to describe what motivates you; in other words, which are your three top drives? Write them in the section provided.

✔ **Find your primary need.** From the three needs you picked, select the one you absolutely must have fulfilled. This top need will be the one that shows up in almost every choice, in almost every way you interact in a relationship. This primary need is one core element of your life purpose. Write it in the section provided.

- *Security.* Are you constantly thinking about how to keep things in control, manageable? Do you always look for options that give you an out? Do you always have (or think you should have) a backup plan? Money in the bank for the future?
- *Expansion.* Are you driven to create more of everything? Do you have big dreams? Want to learn, learn, learn? Want to grow, grow, grow your business?

INVENTORY OF LIFE SATISFACTION
Your Life Wheel
How Well Do You Get Around?

> DIRECTIONS: The eight sections in the wheel represent balance.
> Seeing the center of the wheel as zero and the outer edge as 10,
> rank your level of satisfaction with each area of your life by
> drawing a line, creating a new outer edge (see example). The new
> perimeter of the circle represents the Life Wheel. Imagine how
> bumpy the ride might be if this were a real wheel!

Example:

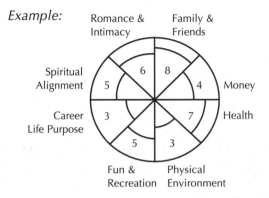

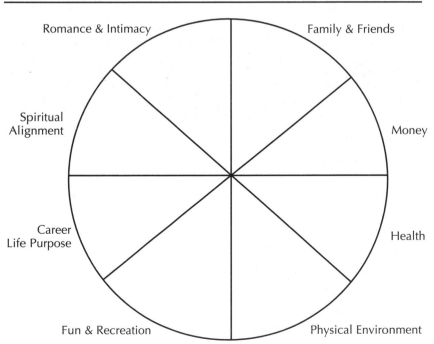

- *Acceptance.* Are you always looking for those subtle signals that people approve of you or like your work? Do you want to be accepted into the major circles in your field? Do you flatter or people-please?
- *Adventure.* Are you constantly chafing at the ordinariness of life, constantly planning your next expedition? Taking risks with other people's money? Leaping before looking? Do you crave exploring the unknown no matter what the field of endeavor?
- *Power.* Are you constantly seeking to be in a better, more powerful position? Do you associate with wealthy or powerful people? Are you generally confident that you can handle most situations — better than others who appear to be too timid? Are you impatient with slow thinkers?
- *Communion.* Do you participate frequently in gatherings of people? Do you gravitate to meetings, congregations, activist groups, like-minded people? Are you so empathic that you can merge with others' thought processes? Do you resist being alone? Are you an organizer?
- *Freedom.* Are you always seeking a way to live by your own time schedule? Can't consider nine-to-five employment as a long-term option? Entrepreneurial? Sole proprietor or talented artist, writer, or performer? Always express different ideas from the norm? Scoff at authorities and institutions? Don't care what people think of you?
- *Expression.* Do you overflow with creative ideas and expression in any form (speaking, writing, art, sculpture, music, doodles, jokes, life-of-the-party antics)? Have you had several professional careers or businesses?
- *Exchange.* Are you passionate about ideas? Always giving out information, sharing insights, looking for like-minded people with whom you can exchange information? Are you always telling people about books you have read, great doctors you have found, good schools, recipes, or better ways to do things?
- *Other.* As you review this list, can you discover a need you have that is not included?

✔ **My three top needs are:**

    1. _____

    2. _____

    3. _____

✔ *My top need is:*

_____

✔ Make a note of your needs on your profile sheet, page 226.

HOW MY TOP NEEDS ARE SHAPING ME: FIVE-MINUTE WRITING EXERCISE

Have your kitchen timer or watch ready, along with your pen. When you are ready to write, set the timer for five minutes or look at your watch. Starting with the top need selected, write, stream-of-consciousness style, on this subject:

[My Top need] shows up in every choice I have made so far. For example. . . . (continue to write without setting any goal).

✔ **As you write:**
- Allow whatever comes out to come out, even if it seems nonsensical.
- Use the words for your other two top needs somewhere in your writing.
- Keep your pen moving until the timer rings!

_____

_____

_____

_____

_____

_____

_____

✔ **After the five minutes are up, stop writing and**
- Notice what word you started with and what word you ended on. Is there a message for you even in these two words?
- Underline significant sentences that give you insight about how your top need is motivating you and shaping your choices.
- Transfer your insights to page 226 of your profile sheet.
- Record insights about your needs on a TIP CARD.

RECOGNIZING MY PRIMARY TYPE

Swiss psychologist Carl Jung described four types of people, based on natural functions in humans, that have since been explored and developed into a well-known personality test by Myers and Briggs. Our life purpose is expressed through our natural style, attitudes, mode of perception, behavior, and worldview.

Look at the descriptions that follow and choose the type that feels most descriptive of you. It's normal to find a little bit of each one in yourself, but if you had to pick just one, which one would it be?

THE FOUR TYPES

■

INTUITIVES—FOCUS ON "WHY?"

"What is the meaning of what I'm doing?"
"How does this relate to the big picture (or to life, philosophy, new trends)?"
"What alternatives and options are there?" "What's the vision?"

■

THINKERS—FOCUS ON "WHAT?"

"What can I learn here?"
"What do we already know?"
"Let's research the facts, and analyze the data."

■

FEELERS—FOCUS ON "WHO?"

"How can I help?"
"Let's discuss this so that it works for everyone."
"Would anyone else like coffee?"

■

DOERS—FOCUS ON "HOW?"

"What can I do?" What does it cost? When do you want it?"
"Let's get on with it! Meetings are a waste of time."

✔ What is your most natural and *dominant* tendency—are you a thinker, doer, feeler, or intuitive?

✔ Transfer your choice to the profile sheet, page 226.

WHAT'S MY LINE?

Answer the following questions to assess how previous jobs fit your natural tendencies.

✔ What job have I had that was *most in line* with my natural tendency (1) to think logically, analyze, and know, (2) to help others, (3) to do and build, or (4) to look for meaning or alternative ways of doing things? _____

_____

✔ What elements did I most like about this job? What was most satisfying? _____

_____

_____

_____

Analysis

✔ Write a synopsis in the space below of what is your "line," and transfer it to page 226 of your profile sheet. (Examples: *I am a thinker who enjoys gathering data and finding the secret information within it that will make a difference in how products are marketed. I'm a big-picture thinker. I'm a people person, and I have to feel I am making a difference in lives. I'm always asking the big cosmic questions about where we're going or what's the point of it all. This workbook is a joke—I know what my purpose is: My purpose is to get up and go to work tomorrow.*)

_____

_____

_____

✔ Write a short fantasy resume, even if you are not looking for a new job, and tuck it away to work its magic in attracting a future opportunity effortlessly! Write this version of your fantasy resume on your profile sheet on pages 226–227 with the other answers from this chapter.

NINE CAREER PATHS

The best way to get a job done is to let the right person do it. As simple as this seems, we sometimes find philosophers building skyscrapers or action people at routine desk jobs. Too often we choose our livelihoods on the basis of the job market. But if you're the communicator who loves to close a sale and go to networking groups, think twice about applying for a job that keeps you in a cubicle staring at a computer, even though programming is hot, hot, hot.

Probably your life purpose can be worked out in more than one way. Even when you find a career that's a perfect fit, remember that every personality type has its blind spots and pitfalls. For example, innovators are usually miles ahead in their thinking, but if they don't take the time to listen to what's needed in a product, they may fall short in reaching their goal. Executives who look only at the bottom line may create such a tough company culture that good people are turned off from working there.

✔ Find the career path that fits you the best from the descriptions that follow.

✔ Make a note of your career path on page 227 of your profile sheet.

Why Do We Go Against Our Grain?

After reading descriptions of the nine career paths, do you find that you have been making money from jobs that you are naturally suited for? If your answer is no, why not?

Have you been working in a situation that allows you to participate from your natural inclination? Or are you a mover and doer who is forced to sit in endless meetings talking about plans or relationships when you just want to get the facts, get organized, and get on with it? Are you a person interested in existential truth but forced to sit and tally up meaningless (to you) statistics? Are you a

> "In the 1980s, I worked for Fortune One Hundred companies. That life was absolutely a reflection of what I believed. I was constantly on the road selling products, living out of a Day-Timer and a suitcase. I had two beliefs that kept me working hard. The first was that I *had* to do this kind of work simply because I was so good at it. . . . I looked . . . very accomplished . . . but the truth was, I was continually exhausted. The second belief was that 'I have to take care of myself.' This fierce belief in total self-sufficiency meant that I lived a very separate-from-God type of life."
>
> —Colleen McGovern,
> in *The Purpose of Your Life*[3]

THE NINE CAREER PATHS

Find the core characteristics of your career identity, perspective, and be
ior by adding together all the numbers in your birthday (e.g., December
1967=1+2+1+4+1+9+6+7=31). Reduce to one digit (e.g., 31=3+1=4). R
the description for your number (in the example given, it would be 4).

1, original, assertive, bold,

charismatic, impulsive, innovative,

focused, inspired, quick, achiever   ] **PIONEER**

Pitfalls: arrogance, impatience, not listening

2, cautious, relationship-oriented,

artistic, nurturing, sensitive,

affectionate, cooperative   ] **NURTURER**

Pitfalls: codependency, overcaution, fear

3, quick thinking, spontaneous,

social, magnetic, gift of gab,

synthesizer, deal-maker   ] **COMMUNICATO**

Pitfalls: prevarication, overoptimism, indulgence

4, pragmatic, systematic planner,

determined, problem-solver,

builder, manager   ] **DOER**

Pitfalls: stubbornness, workaholism, efficiency is God

5, active, magnetic, outgoing,

risk-taker, quick thinker,

unpredictable, entrepreneurial, curious   ] **DISSEMINATOR**

Pitfalls: scattered, unreliable, dilettantism

6, careful, conscientious,
    reliable, nurturing, service/community-
    and family-oriented, traditional   ] **TEACHER**
    Pitfalls: overbearing, smothering, martyrdom

7, innovative, intelligent,
    deep, careful, spiritual, scholar,
    loner, curious, analytical   ] **RESEARCHER**
    Pitfalls: contentious, skeptical, secretive

8, business-like, conservative,
    powerful, analytical, big-picture thinker,
    pragmatic, decision-maker   ] **EXECUTIVE**
    Pitfalls: domineering, cold, judgmental

9, open-minded,
    loves history, literature, arts,
    higher education, long-term, global view   ] **PHILOSOPHER**
    Pitfalls: vagueness, talking, not doing, unmotivated

Note: Your career path number will be expressed by your
    dominant personality type. For example, you could
    be a pioneer in ideas, a pioneer in relationships,
    or a pioneer in physical accomplishments.

thinker who is working in construction but bored building one more identical foundation form?

Somewhere along the line, we begin to notice who's making the big money, who has the big cars, and who has the nice clothes. Before long, we decide that to make money like all the other people we see being so successful, we should be like them! We think, "If I were just more like Sarah, I'd be successful. She's a go-getter. I'll go into sales. I'll learn the secrets of good salesmanship. I'll learn how to be more outgoing and powerfully persuasive." The only problem is, *we* are not naturally outgoing, and the thought of forcing ourselves to be cheerful and "on" all the time is depressing and draining. Or we realize, with disgust, that we don't like the feeling of being manipulated or coerced, so it's going to be pretty hard to motivate ourselves to adopt behaviors that go against our grain. Changing behavior won't work for us if it is not congruent with who we are. Remember, to fulfill your life purpose—by definition—you need not change your identity. For those of us who have tried to diet or exercise, we know how hard it can be to *will* ourselves to be different for long. Instead of willing yourself to be like someone else, concentrate on bringing out more of who you are. Ironically, as you begin to take on new challenges, as you step up to your purpose, your nature will change by itself into a powerful expression of who you really are.

✔ How have I tried to change my nature in the past?

_____

_____

✔ How can I allow more of my true nature to shine forth? Record this answer on page 227 of your profile sheet.

WHAT I LOVE TO DO

✔ Pick three words that best describe what you love to do. Select the one that excites you the most, and write it in the space provided. Continue to write for three minutes about what you love to do, and make sure to include the other two words in the paragraph. Keep your pen moving without stopping.

I love to_____

_____

_____

_____

_____

_____

_____

_____

_____

_____

_____

_____

✔ Review what you wrote, underline what stands out the most, and record your insights on page 227 of your profile sheet.

A COW-PUNCHING PUBLISHER

David Ish, a sixty-year-old native of New Jersey and a Californian since 1976, owns and publishes a free neighborhood newspaper, *The New Fillmore*, in San Francisco. David is a happy example of someone who has found his life purpose, and he lives richly in touch with his passions of poetry, cow-punching, riding elephants in Thailand, water massage, and hanging out with neighborhood friends.

I asked David to talk about how his life purpose unfolded and what insights he might share to help the rest of us.

"Oddly enough, the thing that really opened me up to my path about ten years ago was getting in touch with my body. Being an intellectual, I don't think I had ever really been in my body." David described coming to terms with alcoholism in his late forties, and how he searched for physical and spiritual health. "I studied with various body workers, and began to get in touch with the natural pleasures of the body. Just as an example, one of my teachers told me that when you buy a newspaper, don't just hand over the coin, but turn that money over in your hand and really feel the coin and pay attention to the transaction. Be present. I've never forgotten that simple message. Another teacher taught me to listen to music and feel the micromovements of the body. I studied many body movement techniques, and eventually discovered Watsu, or water massage, of which I'm now a practitioner. Getting in touch with my body opened up my world in a wonderful way.

"The second shift for me was exploring my masculine and feminine sides. After spending time in a men's group and studying about the

> Ask yourself when making decisions, "Does this decision make me feel more open and expanded, or does it make me feel slightly shut down or contracted?" Am I moving toward this idea or away from it?
>
> —*The Purpose of Your Life*[4]

Goddess, I realized I could develop my nurturing side and not have to have a codependent relationship." This was definitely new ground for a man who, in his twenties, was a husband and father doing market research on Wall Street for Fortune 500 companies. "I'd attained a certain level of success in New York, and I got to thinking, 'Is this all there is?' I guess that's when my spiritual quest started."

Leaving behind the corporate world, David lived for a while in British Columbia in a spiritual community that owned a small-town newspaper. As the editor of the paper, his goal was to encourage and stimulate intellectual inquiry. "After three years, I moved down to San Francisco. One day I was having a great discussion about alienation with one of my poet friends—you know only poets can really get into a juicy discussion of alienation—and I said to him, 'You know, what this neighborhood needs is a newspaper.' I remembered that in British Columbia the newspaper created microcelebrities of people in the town. The community was created by the paper. In British Columbia, I was trying to raise the cultural level. Here in San Francisco, we already had plenty of culture, but we needed a feeling of community. Throughout my life I've always seemed to gravitate towards supporting the minority in my milieu, almost regardless of what the minority position was. I now see my life purpose as one of bringing my circumstances more into balance, more into harmony. I even did that in high school and college.

"I've always had an entrepreneurial spirit. In the eighth grade, I started my own newspaper. It was a homeroom daily! I didn't work on the school newspaper, I started my own. I was shut down by the principal because I was doing private business on public property. At twelve and thirteen I got into science fiction, and I published a science fiction fan magazine.

"Starting *The New Fillmore* was totally flawless, with no obstacles. I can't think of another project that was so effortless. The time between getting the idea for it and the first issue rolling off the press was somewhere between forty-five and fifty days. That's all it took for me to go out and sell the ads and print the stories. By then I knew all the aspects of the business—selling, writing, and producing the ads; interviewing people and writing the stories; and producing it through desktop publishing."

At this juncture, all of David's previous experiences in the business world and the world of community building, along with his own personal development, came to bear on his idea and allowed it to come into being effortlessly. "All the people I called on to buy ads already knew me because I shopped in their bakeries, grocery markets, and stores. I wrapped up my previous consulting business and made a seamless transition into the publishing business. I made money from the first issue.

"Each month I'd have a party with the staff, the columnists, and the neighborhood advertisers. The community started coming together. Twelve years later, I still love it. What's elegant about it is that it allows me to make a living and at the same time serve my community. I figured if I couldn't save the world at least I could save the neighborhood.

"I also have to say that, personally, the other thing that makes me feel in balance is my Watsu practice, because it brings in the personal and the body with the broader sense of community. The newspaper and the body work practice make me feel balanced. I have a pretty peaceful existence, so I also make sure that I have something to look forward to that is a break in the routine. I go boogie boarding at the beach. I spend time on a working ranch and go on cattle drives.

"Home! Hauling in the wine, throwing open the shutters, running to water the drooping plants. We settle the wine into crates in the dark wedge of closet under the stairs. The spirit of all the grapes we saw ripening, now bottled and mellowing for those occasions we hope to celebrate. . . . We missed the house and come back understanding the next few circles around us. Qualities those of us with northern blood envy—that Italian insouciance and ability to live in the moment with gusto—I now see came down straight from the Etruscans. All the painted images from the tombs seem charged with meaning, if we only had the clues to read it. I close my eyes and look at the crouching leopards, the deft figure of death, the endless banqueting. Sometimes Greek myths come to mind, Persephone, Actaeon and the dogs, Pegasus, but the instinct I have is that the tomb images—and the Greek ones—each came from further back, and those further back came from something even earlier. The archetypes keep appearing and we find in them what we can, for they speak to our oldest neurons and synapses."

—Frances Mayes[5]

I've been to Thailand and ridden on elephants. I write a column in the paper called The Occasional Traveler, so my travel's even a business write-off as well as an adventure!

"In terms of an overall life purpose, it seems that I have fun doing what I did when I was a kid. I have a friend who says success is doing as an adult what you had fun doing as a kid. As a kid, he always wanted a house with secret rooms. Now he's a science fiction writer with secret rooms in his house.

"I was creating balance in myself. When I was in an intellectual environment that didn't seem social enough, I had to develop my own social skills. On the other hand, when I was in an environment that was lacking in community, I had to develop my skills in developing community. When I was in a community with a low cultural level, I had to deepen my own appreciation of art and literature in depth to share with others."

What Do We Learn from David Ish?
✔ Follow your passions.
✔ Look for what is needed—that you like to do.
✔ Take action.
✔ No experience is ever wasted.
✔ Developing personal and spiritual depth creates a good foundation for right livelihood to grow.
✔ Don't forget to put a good amount of fun into your life!
✔ Never stop experimenting and adventuring.
✔ You might be the person to shift a whole community into balance.

Write any insight you wish to record on your profile sheet on page 227, or write your insights on a TIP CARD.

CHAPTER 4

My Life Story and What It Tells About Me

Yet wherever she goes, her story marches ahead of her. Announces her. Declares and cancels her true self. Oh, she did so want to be happy, but what choice did she have, stepping to the beat of that ragbag history of hers? Of course, the same might be said of the famous Dionne quintuplets, born to an ordinary Canadian farm couple. . . . First there's the children's humble origins to consider. Add to that their miraculous survival, and you've got a story so potent and compelling that the little girls themselves are lost, and will always be lost, that's my opinion, inside its convolutions.

—Carol Shields[1]

YOUR EARLY UPBRINGING IS THE BEGINNING OF YOUR *STORY*

Once upon a time, you were born. Someone might have said, "She looks just like her dad. She looks so intelligent, doesn't she?" And your life began by being surrounded by people looking for signs of your intelligence. Someone might have said, "He's the most stubborn boy. He's a handful." And you thought, "That's right, I'll show them. I'll give them a run for their money." Values and expectations begin to be instilled in us the moment we are born. Necessary conditions constellate and our destiny unfolds, chapter by chapter. In truth, our sacred life purpose *demands* that we see, hear, and be exposed to certain things as reminders of what life tasks lie ahead.

The surrounding conditions—racial, class, economic, cultural, geographic, and emotional—set the stage for our story. We identify ourselves completely with what we might call our "lot in life." Our lot, or our early circumstances, is the "reality" from which our individuality sprouts. David, an officer in the Marines, recalled, "I grew up on a farm. No one in our family ever asked for outside help." Peter, a social

> "No wonder Marcel [Proust] should have felt somewhat unworthy next to his father [an internationally known doctor] . . . He had never harbored any of the professional aspirations that constituted a badge of normality in a late-nineteenth-century bourgeois household. Literature was the only thing he cared for, though he did not, for much of his youth, seem too willing, or able, to write. Because he was a good son, he tried at first to do something his parents would approve of. There were thoughts of joining the Foreign Ministry, of becoming a lawyer, a stockbroker, or an assistant at the Louvre. Yet the hunt for a career proved difficult. ('In my most desperate moments, I have never conceived of anything more horrible than a law office') and the idea of becoming a diplomat was ruled out when he realized it would involve moving away from Paris and his beloved mother. 'What is there left, given that I have decided to become neither a lawyer, nor a doctor, nor a priest . . . ?' asked an increasingly desperate twenty-two-year-old Proust."
>
> —Alain de Botton[2]

worker, said, "I never knew my dad. He disappeared on all of us." Janet, whose parents ran a corner grocery store said, "I had to go to work at fourteen. I never had a social life. I had two kids by age nineteen." Damian, a teacher, said, "Things were bad in our neighborhood, but we stuck together against outsiders." So many scenarios, so many lots. Those scenes, although perhaps long gone from the present moment, continue to shape our thinking about ourselves *and about what is possible*. Maybe, if we are looking for the reason we are here—our life purpose—we don't need a new story but a story that we can feel connected to *now*.

Let's review some of the defining parental beliefs that were going on in Act 1 of your story. As we examine together some of your early history, keep in mind that your soul selected your *particular* mother and father as the two people who best could teach you what you needed to learn at the beginning of life and who would provide exactly the right conditions to nurture certain aspects of your nature (e.g., pushing you to become independent, giving you music lessons; or demonstrating the value of communication and harmony, sometimes through the pain inflicted by demonstrating the very opposite of these values). Jack, who facilitates groups on controlling anger for men, told us, "Yeah, my dad was real violent. I didn't know that other dads didn't hit their kids until I was in late grammar school. I've been so against violence in the home, that I really found my calling in working with men and anger management."

Keep in mind, we are not saying that anyone chose to be beaten regularly or to experience incest. However, according to many traditions, many souls select a life that will provide growth challenges, even though we have no conscious memory of our soul's motivation and, furthermore, cannot imagine how these experiences could have any character-building or redeeming side. If the idea of a soul deliberately choosing a challenging life is repugnant or ridiculous to you, put it aside for now. Continue your examination of the beliefs about the world that were handed down to you by your parents. Our goal here is to find attitudes that are so deeply rooted that they have become your "reality."

Answer the following questions by jotting down your first impressions. If you get stuck on a question, let it go and move on. You might find it interesting to do this exercise again in a few months. More memories or insights may surface later.

The Essence of Your Father

• If there were a caption under a photograph of your father describing his life, what would it say?_____

_____

_____

• What was missing from your father's life? Was there something he wanted to accomplish but didn't do? What characteristics were weakly developed or missing in him?_____

_____

_____

• What were the most important things you learned from him?_____

_____

_____

• How are you like him?_____

_____

_____

• How have you developed in ways that are different?_____

_____

_____

The Essence of Your Mother

• If there were a caption under a photograph of your mother describing her life, what would it say?_____

_____

• What was missing from your mother's life? What did she not do that she wanted to do?_____

_____

• What characteristics were weakly developed or missing in her?_____

_____

• What were the most important things you learned from her?_____

_____

• How are you like her?_____

_____

• How have you developed in ways that are different?_____

_____

Your Parents and God

• What did your parents believe about God?
  *Father*_____

_____

  *Mother*_____

_____

Parental Values and Teachings

• What three values were most important to your parents?
  *Father*_____
  *Mother*_____

• What ideas did your parents most impress on you?

*Father*_____

_____

*Mother*_____

_____

The Positive Purpose of Having Your Specific Parents

• Assuming there was some reason that your parents were the perfect parents for you in this life, what would that reason be?

*Father*_____

_____

_____

*Mother*_____

_____

_____

Combining the Lineages of Your Mother and Father: Who Are You?

• Part of my purpose in life is to integrate my mother's and father's natures and perspectives and take these to another level, which means that_____

_____

_____

_____

✔ On pages 228–229 of the profile sheet write a synopsis of your answer to the preceding question but include ways that you are moving in your own direction.

Parental Beliefs about Money

• Describe briefly how your mother and father each handled money.

_____

_____

_____

_____

• What message about money did you get from your father and your mother?_____

_____

_____

_____

_____

My Beliefs About Money

Write a synopsis of your family's beliefs about money on your profile sheet, p. 228.

Parental Beliefs About Education and Achievement

✔ My father's attitude about education was_____

_____

✔ My father's main expertise was achieved by_____

_____

_____

✔ My father's goal about education for me was best expressed by saying

_____

_____

✔ How was the idea of education talked about in your father's family? Was there any member of his family about whom everyone was very proud? Why? Anyone who was a black sheep? Why? How has the reputation of anyone in your family influenced how you see yourself?

_____

_____

_____

_____

✔ What did your father expect of you? Were his expectations very high, high, average, low, very low?_____

_____

_____

✔ My mother's attitude about education was_____

_____

_____

✔ My mother's main expertise was achieved by_____

_____

✔ My mother's goal about education for me was best expressed by
saying _____

_____

✔ How was the idea of education talked about in your mother's family?
Was there any member of her family about whom everyone was very
proud? Why? Anyone who was a black sheep? Why? How has the reputation of anyone in your family influenced how you see yourself?

_____

_____

_____

✔ What did your mother expect of you? Were her expectations very
high, high, average, low, very low?_____

_____

_____

My Beliefs About Education and Achievement

From your answers to the preceding questions, do you see any pattern
in the expectations that you lived with growing up? If you do, write a
two- or three-sentence synopsis of your insights under the heading
"Beliefs About Education and Achievement" on your profile sheet,
page 228.

Parental Beliefs About Work

• How did your father feel about his work? (Loved it? Hated it?) Why?

_____

_____

• What did your father say about work that you still remember?_____

_____

_____

• Do you think your father was fulfilled in his work? _____

_____

_____

• What was your father best at doing? _____

_____

• Was your father an entrepreneur? A corporate man? A blue-collar worker?_____

_____

• What did you think about the work your father did?_____

_____

• Did your father support the ideas you had about your future? _____

_____

• What did your mother feel about your dad's work? (Loved it? Hated it?) Why? What did he feel about her work? _____

_____

• What did your mother feel about her own work? (Loved it? Hated it?) Why? _____

_____

• What did your mother say about work that you still remember? _____

_____

• Do you think your mother was fulfilled in her work? _____

_____

• What was your mother best at doing? _____

_____

• Was your mother an entrepreneur? A corporate woman? A blue-collar worker? A homemaker? _____

• What did you think about the work your mother did? _____

_____

• Did your mother support the ideas you had about your future? _____

_____

_____

My Beliefs About Work

In looking at the memories you have about your family and work, do you see any pattern of beliefs that is still in place today? Write one, two, or three sentences that synopsize this section under the heading "Beliefs About Work" on the profile sheet, on page 228.

My Beliefs About My Ability in Comparison to Others'

✔ What did you hear about yourself when you were growing up (especially about your abilities and probabilities for success in the future) from:

Teachers? _____

_____

_____

Parents? _____

_____

_____

Siblings? _____

_____

_____

Other family members? _____

_____

_____

Neighbors? _____

_____

_____

✔ What was the best thing you ever heard someone say about you?

_____

✔ What was the most hurtful thing you ever heard someone say about you? _____

_____

Unconscious Ceilings

✔ How has either of the last two answers affected your sense of yourself?

_____

_____

✔ Do you think either of these two answers is definitive of who you are?
_____

✔ What are your criteria for success? _____
_____
_____
_____

✔ How close are you to being successful? (25%? 80%? 110%?)
_____

✔ Circle the words that best describe who you are when dealing with money: Are you vague, aggressive, tight-fisted, impulsive, helpless, generous, practical, penny-pinching, fair, carefree, suspicious, optimistic, careless, manipulative, price-conscious, or hoarding?

✔ Are you fearful of being a bag lady? Are you an excellent planner? A saver? Do you enjoy the challenge of working for yourself or on commission because of the potential? Does money always "show up" for you at the right time? _____
_____
_____

✔ If money were a person you were in a relationship with, which of the following control dramas would best describe you? _____
_____
_____

• Would money be an *intimidator*? (You feel your survival is threatened.) _____
_____
_____

• Would money be an *interrogator*? (You feel bad because you don't think you handle money shrewdly.) _____
_____
_____

• Are you *aloof* about money? (You don't keep a checkbook balance. You have no idea what your income tax will be.) _____
_____
_____

• Are you a *victim* concerning money? (You constantly complain about lack of money and feel helpless to bring in what you need for living expenses.) _____
_____

• *Other?* _____

✔ Which of the nine career paths are you following now? (See Chapter 2, pages 32–33: the pioneer, nurturer, communicator, doer, disseminator, teacher, researcher, executive, or philosopher.)_____

_____

✔ Do you love what you're doing? _____

_____

✔ What change would like to make in your livelihood? _____

_____

_____

✔ List everything you would have to do to go into a new field (if applicable).

_____

_____

_____

✔ What do you want from your livelihood in terms of money?

_____

_____

_____

✔ How much money can a person in your field or educational bracket earn? _____

_____

✔ What is it costing you not to make any changes in your life right now?

_____

_____

_____

✔ Reread your answers to the preceding questions. Jot down any further insights here.

_____

_____

_____

_____

✔ Reread your answers in a week or a month. Jot down any further insights here.

_____

_____

_____

_____

✔ Write down anything you want to be part of your profile sheet on page 229 or write insights on a TIP CARD.

MIND-MAPPING YOUR DREAMS AND GOALS

A simple but effective process for exploring all the corners of your beliefs about your dreams and goals is mind-mapping. You can, within a few minutes, gain tremendous insight about your life path by laying out on a piece of paper your goal, what you believe about that goal, what you think you have to do to achieve that goal, and specific actions to take. Just by doing this exercise you begin to awaken and activate your inner navigator. You begin to see that anything is possible. Review the mind map example on page 51. Don't make this exercise difficult; simply start to lay out your own mind map on the blank mind map on pages 52–53, or use a separate sheet of paper.

How to Start Your Mind Map
✔ Write the issue that you wish to work under "What I want to create."
✔ In the upper left corner, write down any goals you wish to achieve concerning this issue.
✔ In the middle right, list everything you think is stopping you from succeeding.
✔ As you think about either your goals on the upper left or your obstacles on the middle right, you may have intuitive ideas that pop up in terms of "Things to do/Check out." List those ideas or action steps on the upper left. List limiting parental beliefs and what you *think* limits you. Jot down the roots of your beliefs.

Things to do/Check out
Analysis
✔ Review your answers in the preceding mind-mapping exercise.
✔ What *actions* would you have to take to move toward your goals? For example, a woman named Jackie was an accountant who wanted to be a naturopathic doctor. She began to save money, looked for a school of naturopathy, and talked to other practitioners about the field. She also practiced imagining herself in a light-filled office, surrounded by books and remedies, seeing patients.
✔ What are your beliefs about yourself and your goals? In Jackie's case, she said she had to overcome the belief that since she was such a good accountant, she should stay in that field to make good money even though her heart wasn't in it anymore.

MIND-MAPPING EXAMPLE

GOALS

- Have my own business.
- Need to make $35,000/year.
- Would like an experienced business partner.
- I want a beautiful, serene atmosphere.
- I see myself standing near the front door, greeting people.

My dream is to own a small teahouse, but I don't have any business experience.

I'm not sure it's the right goal.

OBSTACLE
"Fear" "Uncertainty"

THINGS TO DO/CHECK OUT

- Who can counsel me about business?
- Put ad in newspaper for business partner. See who shows up.
- Get info: Treat like another "assignment" from my boss!"
- Share my dream with positive people.
- How is "being rejected by my father" an advantage in getting what I want in my present situation?

BELIEFS I HAVE ABOUT MY OBSTACLE

- My family thought making money was greasy.
- I'm not good at business.
- I'm lacking something.
- I won't make enough quickly to live on.
- I'm not organized.

Am I willing to believe something different/positive?

ROOTS OF MY PROBLEM

- I've always worked for others.
- I felt invisible as a child.
- My parents both had "victim of life" mentalities.
- My father was disappointed I was born a girl and not a boy.
- Neither parent was in business.

All these experiences had a purpose!

MIND MAPPING HOW TO GET FROM HERE TO WHERE I'D LIKE TO BE

Short-Term Goals

_____
_____
_____
_____
_____
_____
_____
_____
_____
_____
_____
_____
_____
_____
_____
_____

Things to do/Check out

_____
_____
_____
_____
_____
_____
_____
_____
_____
_____
_____
_____
_____
_____
_____
_____

What I want to create

_____
_____
_____
_____
_____
_____
_____

Parental beliefs that may be limiting me

_____
_____
_____
_____
_____
_____
_____
_____
_____

What I think prevents me from having what I want

_____
_____
_____
_____
_____
_____
_____
_____

"Roots" of my problem. Where did my limiting beliefs come from?

_____
_____
_____
_____
_____
_____
_____

✔ What would you like the universe to provide for you? Jackie said that once she made up her mind to change fields, she received a phone call from an old friend who was willing to share her house, which was near the school she wanted to attend. Soon after moving, she found a part-time job as an accountant to help her through school.

✔ Make a list of what you are willing to do to reach your goals and what you'd like the universe to do.

What I Will Do   What I Want the Universe to Do

_____   _____
_____   _____
_____   _____
_____   _____
_____   _____
_____   _____
_____   _____

Congratulations! Now that you have completed your mind map, you should have a much clearer picture of where you are and how to move forward. If so, record any insights on a TIP CARD.

MY PERSONAL TIME LINE

Directions:

✔ To help you draw your own time line, read Dianne Aigaki's brief story, which follows, and her time line of milestone influences. As you will see, she selected the events in her life that clarified, defined, or helped birth parts of her life purpose.

✔ Next, reflect on your own history. What events, people, or influences stand out for you? Fill in your time line (on the page following Dianne's), representing your own milestones, defining moments and influences, and turning points so far. As you jot these down on your time line, consider how these influences have reflected your life purpose in some way. Do you see any patterns or common themes in what has influenced you?

✔ When you finish your time line, you may find it fun to write a short "fairy story" based on the story of your life on your profile sheet, page 228.

DIANNE'S STORY

Dianne Aigaki, an artist, psychologist, and grant writer, splits her time between the Napa Valley in California and Dharamsala, India, where she works with the Tibetan government-in-exile. "My life has always been about service to others," Dianne said in her characteristically buoyant style. "I've always found time to volunteer.

"The best description of my life now is the feeling that all of the things I have been and done in my life have come together in Dharamsala. My skills as an artist and a grant writer, and my decades of experience in community work of all kinds, fit in very well with what is needed and wanted in the Tibetan exile community. And what I want for the rest of my life is exemplified in the Tibetan people and how their government operates. The picture I have is that all of my life's experiences so far have been funneled into, magnetized into, the Tibetan community. The funnel then reverses, so that all the fine qualities they bring are poured back into me. I'm at this incredibly lucky point in my life, where what I have to offer in terms of skills matches what they need, and what I want to learn and become is matched by what they have to teach me."

Dianne's life purpose has emerged in several distinct ways. "I grew up in a Midwestern family where people never talked about their feelings. Everyone was very nice but controlled in terms of anger and hesitant to share any of the ups and downs, ins and outs, of their emotional life. That early influence colored my whole approach to life. I became the person who primed other people to value and tell their story, and I learned to value and tell my own. Becoming a psychologist taught me the necessity and power of telling your story and not being afraid to do that.

"With my dear friend Barbara Morse, I began a family history project called 'Tell Us Your Story,' fifteen years ago. In one afternoon, we developed a list of twenty-five questions that we felt really got at the crux of people's life passages, and turned these questions into family history workshops, a school curriculum, and community festival events. We realized that these questions crossed generational, cultural, and gender boundaries, and reached the heart of everybody's life story. Anybody anywhere can answer these questions—questions like 'How did your life change after you had a baby?' 'How did your life change after someone close to you died?' 'What did someone teach you that made a difference?' And our favorite question, which is 'What family secret did you learn that changed your view of yourself or someone in your family?'

"I used this question once when I was at the home of my friend Michael. There were two other visitors—two very shy guys from North Dakota—waiting for Michael to come home. They sat on the couch patiently and politely for hours without talking to me or each other. Finally, I went over and said, 'Hey, have either of you learned a family secret that changed your view of yourself or someone in your family?' They both said yes, and we immediately had a wonderful conversation of extremely intimate information. One of the guys, Darren, told how his father had killed someone in a fight as a young man and had become very inward and fearful of his emotions after that event. Darren had just learned this, and it answered a lifetime of questions for him—he had modeled himself after his shy, withdrawn father without knowing the story behind his father's personality. By the time Michael came home, the three of us were on our way to being dear friends.

"In 1987, for Barbara's birthday, we took the twenty-five questions from the 'Tell Us Your Story' project and had people answer them in thirty countries around the world all on one day. I took the questions to China. In Shanghai I posted them in a public park, and hundreds of people came all day long and wrote their answers. Some people came up to me with tears in their eyes. They said they'd never thought they'd see Chinese people in public daring to talk about personal thoughts and feelings. On a thirty-hour boat trip up the Pearl River, we handed out blank books with the questions at the top of the page. At first people were hesitant to take the books or write their answers, but within a short time hundreds of people all up and down the aisles were lying on their bunk beds, looking over each other's shoulders, reading what each person had written and telling their own stories.

"A man who spoke English came up to me and said, 'The woman sitting across from you is a teacher. She wants you to know she has answered all of the questions, and she has written a poem that she wants me to read out loud." People from all over the boat came to stand and hear the poem. The poem said, 'When we all got on the boat at Guangzhou yesterday, we were strangers and afraid of each other. Because you have given us these questions to answer, and we have dared to tell our stories, we will be friends and family forevermore.' "

The reaction of the Chinese people was excitement everywhere Dianne went; they were charmed and heartened by the project. The Chinese police, however, felt differently. Dianne spent several days being interrogated by the police as they tried to determine why she had come to China to ask these questions, who had paid for the trip, who wanted to know the answers, and what was the ulterior motive that would bring someone halfway around the world to ask people personal questions. Finally, Dianne gave the policemen one of the scrolls with the question, "Who named you and what does your name mean?" After a few minutes of conversational interchange among them, smiles and laughter broke out as they related to each other who had named them and what their names meant. A few minutes later, Dianne was free to go.

Strangely enough, Dianne's strong connection with the Chinese people now has another arena in which to be played out. "Living now among the Tibetan people and working with the government-in-exile, I find that I function as a healing bridge because of my positive experience in China with the Chinese people. The faith I have in their intentions as compassionate human beings is part of what I bring to the Tibetans. Faith and compassion will be needed in order to realize a free Tibet.

"I find, because of my experiences in China, that I can express thoughts about the Chinese people that many Tibetans hope to be true. Their future depends on that possibility—that the Chinese can also deal with people in a compassionate and just way."

How did Dianne come to leave her artist's studio and life as a grant writer in the Napa Valley, and suddenly take up residence at the foot of the Himalayas in northern India?

"A few years ago, I traveled to Dharamsala with a group who were students of Tibetan Buddhism. Although I was not a Buddhist myself, a friend of mine was part of this group. I had a synchronistic experience which led me to believe that I should go. The same day that I heard my friend was going, someone else called to tell me that the Dalai Lama and I have the same birthday, July 6. Within the hour, I sent in my deposit for the trip! After arriving there, I was instantly drawn to the dynamics of the community and the struggles and aspirations of the Tibetan government. I was thrilled with the idea that I could live in a community, and in a nation where the leader was an impeccable moral authority. I began to really yearn to live in a country where the people aspire to be like the leader. From there it seemed very simple. I realized it wasn't a fantasy. Here was a place that I could live where service to others is the theme of the society. I could live in a community where the mandate of the government is for people to behave in what I consider to be the highest ways that people can live with each other—with compassion and kindness for others. It is expected that everyone is constantly functioning to the highest code. Tibetans don't operate from the idea of the lowest common denominator. What a difference it is! I feel completely like myself there. I feel like I am becoming a better person by osmosis from those around me. It's not just something I'm reading about. And I don't have to fight against the predominant themes of the culture—consumerism, fear, and stress at the expense of joy and peace. I don't have to fight the prevailing mentality of short-term aspirations and short-term gains. The Dalai Lama is the head of my government, my boss and my neighbor—what could be better?"

DIANNE'S TIME LINE

A review of the milestones of Dianne's life reveals an emerging life purpose.

1. Born to midwestern, kind and loving, but noncommunicative parents. Father described himself as an "honest man," rather than in terms of his job title.
2. Was very close to three self-made, high-powered, charming aunts who chose to live together and not marry; excellent role models of grace, kindness, and open-mindedness.
3. Aunts taught that as a woman, you can have anything you want. Instilled a strong sense of community and the value of relationships with women.
4. Age 18—went to Brazil with $40 and a one-way ticket. Was director of a binational center. Got involved with third-world politics, and saw effect of U.S. intervention and corporate meddling. Effect: politicized her.

5. Brazil trip served as a reference point throughout her life: "If I could live and thrive there at such a young age on virtually nothing, I could do anything."

6. Age 21—felt she was too eccentric, so she married a quiet, conservative man.

7. Age 22—got a master's degree in clinical psychology. "It gave me instant credibility, and provided a lifelong useful skill."

8. Late 20s—Divorced. Realized dream of living on an island. Rented cabin on an island in the Sacramento Delta; pursued art and psychology, and was the assistant director of a planetarium. "I had huge parties with my friends and turned on the stars for them. I'm pretty good at identifying what is fun for me to do and then bringing in my friends to do it with me."

9. Age 31—decided to have a child with my best friend, who was seven years younger. We both committed to being 50 percent responsible for finances and care of our daughter. We've all maintained a wonderful relationship.

10. Wrote and published a book on couples who break up after the birth of a baby.

11. Developed my ability to write grants and translate people's visions for community needs into funding.

12. Continued to maintain old relationships and develop new ones.

13. Developed artistic expression through painting and printmaking.

14. Designed and produced a line of greeting cards that are executed by at-risk teens and teen parents.

15. Moved to an island without electricity or water in the Napa River; lived there seven years: "I needed solitude, and it allowed me to have a physical adventure with the elements—the water and my boat. It was calming and exhilarating at the same time."

16. Went to India. Left the island; sold everything; now live ten months a year in Dharamsala and write grants and train grant writers for the Tibetan government-in-exile.

MY STORY AS A FAIRY TALE

Go ahead. Take a stab at writing a short, funny description of your life as if you were telling it to a five-year-old as a bedtime story. Watch those creative images roll out as you dramatize your life to the present moment. Give your story a perfect title, like forty-three-year-old Janine's *The Girl with Her Nose in a Book*; twenty-six-year-old Zack's *The Spider Boy Who Grew Up to Handle Anything*; or *The Girl Who Saves the World from Her Home*, by a fifty-seven-year-old journalist researching ecological news.

How would you describe yourself without referring to what you do for a living?

I am _____

_____

_____

_____

_____

Transfer the most important descriptions of yourself to your profile sheet on page 228.

MY OBITUARY—WHY NOT NOW?

If you died tomorrow, what would your friends and relatives have to say about you? Many obituaries are short, but they are filled with names of loved ones with whom many precious hours were spent and many projects attempted and completed. Other death notices are testimonies to a vast range of human achievements, failures, and contributions. Following are three examples. Notice the information included: name, birthdate, place of birth, parental heritage, notable accomplishments, contributions to specific fields (film, music, art, literature, education, medicine, science), and the list of family and friends. Go ahead. Write your own. Then you may want to write an additional paragraph describing what you would have liked to achieve before you leave your body! Be bold. Your affirmation for future deeds may well open the way for their accomplishment!

MURRAY, JAKE—His soul peacefully left his shell on October 16, 1998 in Fair Oaks, CA. He was 12. Forever in the hearts of those who had the pleasure to cross paths with him. Jake loved to play, was very mischievous, loving, sensitive, psychic, intelligent, giving, friendly and the most handsome boy. Jake loved to cuddle, pat you gently on your face and knead his Mamma's head. He is survived by his mother, Beth, who he knew deeply adored and loved him; his brother, Montana; Grandma Dee; Grandpa Dennis; Auntie Denise; uncles Barry, Doug, Scott & Jeff; and his favorite playmates, Ella, Melinda, Lefty, Pete, Dakota, Terri, Julie, and many other "kiddies" on the block and throughout CA.

His existence with us and the times we will soon share with him when our souls cross again, will be celebrated Sunday, October 25, 1998. Jake will never be forgotten, he can never be replaced and the memories of his life will bring us joy, love and laughter forever! We will always love you Jake. Thank you for coming into our lives and you will be ooohhhhh soooooo missed!!!!!!! Oh, how the "thunder roars" in a star studded, cloudless night.[3]

My Obituary

_____

_____

_____

_____

_____

_____

_____

_____

_____

_____

_____

_____

_____

_____

_____

Stud "The Kid" Ungar won the World Series of Poker in 1980, 1981, and 1997, the year he defeated more than three hundred competitors to take home a $1.1 million pot. He once lost $1 million in a single craps session and dropped hundreds of thousands of dollars in no-limit poker games. Mr. Ungar suffered from numerous health problems, sometimes winning poker tournaments while in agony from stomach ailments. He became a top gin rummy player while growing up in New York City, where his father ran a bar. He learned to play poker after moving to Las Vegas in the 1970s.[4]

What purpose might Mr. Ungar's life story reveal?

Bessie Cohen, one of the last survivors of New York's infamous garment district fire at the Triangle Shirtwaist Co., almost 88 years ago, died at age 107. The former seamstress, who suffered from Parkinson's disease and limited hearing, was honored three years ago by the Union of Needletrades, Industrial and Textile Employees, UNITE, and the Jewish Home for the Aging on the 85th anniversary of the March 25, 1911, tragedy.

The historic fire in the 10-story garment factory on Manhattan's Lower East Side killed at least 146 workers and promoted some of the first worker safety laws in the country.

Reports of the Triangle fire claimed that exits to the building were sealed either to keep seamstresses from stealing or to prevent union organizers from entering the building to foster a strike. Whatever the reason, many workers were trapped and died.

Completing a nine-hour shift that March afternoon, Ms. Cohen ran down eight flights of stairs to escape. Bessie Gabrilowich (later Cohen) was a 19-year-old Jewish immigrant from Russia who had been in the United States for only three years. Her wages were $3 a week.

She went on to work in a grocery store, marry and move to Connecticut and, in 1941, to Los Angeles, where she settled.

But she lived all her life with nightmares of the fire—of trips to the morgue to identify co-workers' bodies and particularly of a friend's facial expression before she leaped to her death.

"Everybody was running, trying to get out," Ms. Cohen told the *Los Angeles Times* in 1996, "And there was this beautiful little girl, my friend, Dora. I remember her face before she jumped."

Dora Wolfovitch was 15, earning $2.50 a week, and had just decided to take Ms. Cohen's advice to ask for a raise when she died in the fire.

UNITE considered Ms. Cohen and the long-ago Triangle fire symbols of safety problems in the garment industry that the union says
continue today.[5]

Dame Iris Murdoch, whose macabre yet comic sensibility made
her one of Britain's most admired modern novelists . . . Dame Murdoch had a background in philosophy and her fiction grappled with
such questions as the nature of good and evil . . . many of [her] novels are exuberantly melodramatic, offering bemused records of
romantic or erotic follies, as well as more somber battles between
individuals representing moral good and its opposite. Characters,
drawn largely from the middle class, are described with loving exac-
titude and in such depth that their struggles to define what it means
to live a good life take on dramatic force. Before beginning to teach
at Oxford, she spent a year at Cambridge studying with disciples of
the Austrian philosopher Ludwig Wittgenstein. In 1956, she married
John Bayley [an academic, critic, and writer who shared her life for
more than 40 years]. In a 1994 interview, [this prize-winning novel-
ist] said two of the most important things in her life were her parents
and her work. "But above all else, the most important thing in my
life is my husband," she said. "To have had a happy marriage is a
very good thing."[6]

CHAPTER 5

Getting Past Resistances

The great thing about this kind of work is that every feeling that you have, every negative feeling, is in a way precious. It is your building material, it's your stone, it's something you use to build your work. I would say the conversion of the negative is very important. So I taught to myself what I try to teach my students who are becoming writers: Don't duck pain. It's precious, it's your gold mine, it's the gold in your mine.

—RICHARD STERN[1]

COMMON MISTAKES THAT HOLD US BACK FROM FINDING LIFE PURPOSE

The following misconceptions about what life purpose is and "where" it is tend to make us feel discouraged or even hopeless about ever getting on track. Review these common mistakes and see if some part of you has been thinking along these lines. By becoming aware of these misperceptions, you can free yourself of their limitations. By feeling the exciting possibility of each moment, you naturally become purposeful and confident, with the *immediate* ability to make new choices that connect you to your purpose in *this* moment.

Four Common Mistakes
1. *Life purpose is a job title.* "I just have to find the right job to be happy."
2. *Life purpose is far away in time.* "It will probably take me about five years (or some fixed period of time) to get my life together."

3. *Life purpose has to be discovered "out there."* We turn to career counselors or other people to tell us what it is, rather than looking within for what we like to do.
4. *We have to become a different person to be successful.* We've all had the experience of feeling inadequate, as if we are not as lucky or talented as other people. We make judgments such as *The only way to be credible is to get a Ph.D. I'm too shy to be really successful. I'm not aggressive enough to be competitive.* And so on.

Four Common Beliefs That Obscure Life Purpose, and How to Work Through Them

"I don't know what my passion is."

Some of us are enthusiastic and openly "passionate" about life, and we know exactly what we want to do. Others are less expressive, quieter, and reflective or analytical. If you are the type who doesn't feel any strong passion, here are two things that you can do to help define your interests if not your bliss:

✔ **Pay attention to your thoughts, daydreams, and interests.** Do what Joseph Campbell, the great mythologist and writer, was told to do at age twenty by philosopher Ernest Holmes. Write down everything that interests you for the next month. See if a pattern emerges. Use pages 131–133 in Chapter 9 for tracking your interests. Once you've tracked your thoughts for thirty days, review your notes and summarize the pattern of interests you have found on page 229 of your profile sheet.

✔ **Review your high points.** What activities or jobs in the past really excited you? Are they still important to you? Of all the things you are involved in now, what one or two things stand out as highly important to you? Add these to your notes on the profile sheet, page 229.

✔ **Describe someone you admire.** This list will be a description of things *you* would like to do, too. Watch your tendency to think, "Oh, but they are special. I'm not like that." What could you do to explore or develop these characteristics in yourself *today?*

"I need clarity about my life purpose before I do anything new."

✔ **Give up clarity and be willing to live in uncertainty.** I believe that clarity is a trap! Oddly enough, clarity is often spelled by us in our minds this way—GUARANTEE. By waiting for this so-called clarity to come, we remain just where we are—stuck and paralyzed.

✔ **Know that you are where you need to be today.** Instead of waiting for clarity, which incidentally almost never comes until after you've taken some action, I suggest that you focus on staying in the moment. Give up any tendency to blame your situation on the past or on others. In other words, give up being a victim in your thinking. Assume that you are in the exact place you need to be (either you had to learn a certain lesson or your choices were the best you could make at the time). Describe how your world is a perfect staging point for you right now, and transfer this thought to page 230 of your profile sheet.

✔ **Keep developing your interests.** Don't wait to make up your mind about piano lessons or saxophone lessons until you've tried a little of each. Most often you need experience to get clarity. Instead of waiting for clarity, ask to be shown the best opportunity available at this moment. Ask for the next step to be made as clear as possible, and then move toward it. Be willing to live in uncertainty and to let go of the need to know.

"I'm so scattered I don't know which way to go."
Also, "I can't afford to make any changes" (because of money, family ties, lack of skills, and so on).

> **"This troubling paradox of needing a dream to inspire us, yet finding that its fulfillment leaves us perplexed and empty, is vitally significant from the perspective of the Stages of the Soul. For in spiritual terms, we need both elements, the hope and the disillusionment, to see things clearly."**
>
> —Harry R. Moody[2]

✔ **Simplify and focus on the feeling you want.** Don't be afraid to take a "day" job or part-time job while you explore possibilities more dear to your heart. It's hard to develop your latent abilities or interests when you fear for your day-to-day survival. However, if you are thrashing around with five or six potential projects, you are probably not going to be successful with any one of them until you make a commitment to following through on something.

✔ **Determine what you most need right now.** Stability? Freedom? Try to make a choice that includes both stability and freedom. Focus your thinking along the lines of a statement such as *Life just keeps getting better and better.* Always write your statement as if you already had what you want. Don't use negative terms like *I want to get rid of my horrible boss.* Instead, write *I'm working with a group of exceptionally creative and fun people who appreciate my work.*

✔ **Write your statement here** and write it again on page 230 of your profile sheet. _____

_____

_____

_____

"It's hard for me to find my life purpose because of (past woes)."

✔ **Resist the temptation to blame.** Most of us have a tendency to justify our problems by blaming them on our past or other people. We feel if only we'd done this or that, or had this or that, we'd be further along. Giving up the victim stance is one of the most profoundly effective ways we can regain our power.

TURN PROCRASTINATION INTO INFORMATION AND ACTION

In Chapter 1 we looked at the points of the Oprah story that revealed an underlying process based on a misidentification of what was required in the situation and the resulting fear, which produced a ceiling on the expectations of success. As we search for clarification about what our purpose in life is, we can start anywhere and still zero in on the important information that will move us forward *now*. We don't have to limit ourselves to a linear approach (e.g., write out a job resume, search the classifieds for the right fit, look in college catalogues), all of which are necessary sometimes. Instead, we can start anywhere with any of the principles outlined in this book. In Maggie's story, which follows, we started by defining one project on which she was procrastinating.

Often the process of looking for the meaning of an event produces an insight that matters. That insight will prompt the recognition of some new action or behavior that is within our ability to perform. Then we move forward, often exponentially in comparison to the seemingly insignificant nature of the original event. Such was the case with Maggie, a forty-nine-year-old woman who quit a high-level office administration job in a corporate law office to start her own freelance office-assisting business. Read her story and then fill out the blank exercise at the end of the example.

MAGGIE'S STORY

CA: Maggie, is there any project that you want to do or are planning to do but haven't yet moved on?

MAGGIE: Yes, definitely. I want to do my invoicing of clients on Quick-Books within the next month. After I get that set up, then I want to enter all my expenses and income into the system so I can give it to a bookkeeper and eventually figure out the taxes for next year.

CA: Why have you not done this yet?

MAGGIE: Well, it's been sitting there in piles. It's all there. I just need to move it into a routine so that it gets done each month.

CA: How does it feel to you sitting there?

MAGGIE: It feels like a drain.

CA: Why have you not done this yet? (I repeated this question several times in order to get all her layers of reasons why she had not done it yet.)

MAGGIE: [1] It's funny, because I do this for others. But when I get home at the end of the day, I'm too tired to get down to doing it for myself. [2] Things to do with money are always hard for me. I'm too tired to deal with it. [3] I've been taking on too much work. I feel driven and tired, and this pile is a low priority. [4] I have to do things which bring in money. Doing these receipts and invoices doesn't

> **HOW TO GAIN INNER POWER**
>
> Breathe and get centered.
> Bring your attention to *now*.
> Trust your next decision.
> Take a new step.
> Review failures for lessons.
> Spend some time in nature.
> Get enough sleep.
> Do what matters most.
> Stop trying to control things on the outside.
> Get a bigger perspective.
> Use your sense of humor.
> Do your best at all times.
> Do less. Be more.
> Simplify.

bring in money. [The irony is that invoicing is a task that does bring in money!]

CA: What is your internal dialogue about putting your invoices, expenses, and income on QuickBooks?

MAGGIE: I tell myself that when I finish my clients' projects, then I can get started on mine. They are the priority. That's what pays the bills.

CA: What do you think you do in the world as a person? What might people say you do? Who do people see you as?

MAGGIE: You know, I hear all the time how calm I am. I mean, some-times—obviously, I'm not always calm. But I guess I'd have to say I calm people down, whether it's organizing things, inspiring people about something, or having them see a new perspective.

CA: Who are you today—on this date? What do you like about your life?

MAGGIE: I'm a woman. I work for myself, even though I haven't done my consulting business for a long time. I feel I have demonstrated being self-reliant, although of course I could always be more so. I love my son and I adore all my friends. Actually, I feel I'm a power-ful woman, even though I have far to go, and in comparison to some maybe not that powerful. I know that power comes from a higher source. I love life and I'm committed to growing.

CA: Are you aware of how you often say something positive about your-self and then immediately downplay that strength?

MAGGIE: No! I never thought about that before. Do I do that? I guess I do!

CA: So let's assume that your not putting the bookkeeping on Quick-Books may not be the real issue. What do you think is the real issue of not doing the bookkeeping?

MAGGIE: It feels that the issue may be that I am not fully stepping into my power. By having it hanging over my head, I feel drained and guilty about not getting to it.

CA: What is the result of not doing it?

MAGGIE: It keeps me feeling uneasy, fearful.

CA: What is the end result of not doing it?

MAGGIE: I'm in the dark about the state of my finances.

CA: Exactly. By not entering in the figures, you don't have to look at how your business is doing, right?

MAGGIE: Exactly. And I do feel fearful that maybe the bottom line will be that I need to make more money and that my business isn't going to survive and I'll have to go back to work for somebody else.

CA: So you rationalized being too tired to do it, putting everyone else's priority ahead of your own so that you could keep yourself in the dark about the state of your cash flow? At the same time, you were reinforcing the belief that making money is hard work and proving that because you are so tired. If you look at what you said you "do" in the world, it's calm people down whether it is organizing, inspiring them, or getting them to see a new perspective. If that's so, then maybe doing their bookkeeping is not the level of work that is really on purpose for you. Maybe you need to actually do the work you were born to do by organizing them for a month and then hiring them a bookkeeper to do the actual detail work, and you move on to the next client—or continue to do metaorganizing tasks for them.

MAGGIE: Wow. I never thought of that. Looking at it that way would alleviate the driven feeling I have to handle these million details. I really can't continue with the pace I've set for myself. I'm getting up at 5 a.m. to meditate, and I'm usually still working until 8 or 9 o'clock.

CA: It sounds like you are still operating on the paycheck-to-paycheck mentality you had as a driven, conscientious office assistant. Like many of us, you have misidentified the true nature of your task and purpose in the world.

MAGGIE: I thought I had to do it all.

CA: There's a belief! Has anything been coming into your life lately that relates to your feelings, anything that you can see as a message or a solution? It's usually something right in front of us.

MAGGIE: [Laughing sheepishly] Yeah, my neighbor next door is on disability and she asked me yesterday, "Is there anything I could help you with? You seem so busy all the time!"

CA: So what do you think about that?

MAGGIE: I could have her do some cleaning for me. I could even have her do some of the prep work on the bills so that it would be easier for me to enter on the QuickBooks. I wouldn't even have to do it all in one night.

CA: Now you're talking.

TWENTY QUESTIONS FOR
TRANSFORMING PROCRASTINATION

✔ *Fill in the answers to the questions below. Don't think too much. Do this exercise quickly, and let the first answers or impressions come through. If at all possible, do this exercise with a friend. Have the friend read you each question and record your answers. Then exchange with your friend and ask him or her the questions.*

Where You Are Stuck

✔ Pick one specific project that you want to do in the next week or month. Describe the project in detail. _____
_____
_____
_____

• Why have you not done this yet? _____
_____
_____

• How does it feel to you to leave this project undone? _____
_____
_____

• Why have you not done this yet? (Yes, answer this one again.) _____
_____
_____

• What is your internal dialogue about doing this specific project?

Your Innate Power

• What do you think you do in the world as a person? What do people say you are good at? Who do people see you as? (For example, "People say I calm them down." "I'm often told that I'm fun to be around." "I'm very energetic and always get things done on time.")
_____
_____

• When you have completed this project, what will that mean about you? _____
_____

Secondary Gains from Procrastinating

- Assume that your reason for procrastination is not the real issue. What might be the real reason for not working on your project?

  _____

  _____

- What is the consequence of not doing this?

  _____

  _____

- What will you have to give up in order to do the project?

  _____

  _____

- What does the incomplete project keep you from doing?

  _____

  _____

- What fear might you be avoiding by not doing this?

  _____

  _____

The Belief That Stopped You

- What do you want? _____

  _____

- What stops you from getting it? _____

  _____

  _____

- If that problem were taken care of, what else would stop you?

  _____

  _____

  _____

- Your answers to the preceding two questions are your *beliefs* about whether you can have what you want. What are these beliefs?

  _____

  _____

  _____

  _____

The Next Step

- Move into the time and place where you have the satisfaction and fulfillment of completing the project on which you have been procrastinating. (Imagine where you are at the time, what is happening around you, and what scenario you are experiencing. Write down a few notes about what you see, hear, smell, and feel.) _____

  _____

  _____

- Now imagine what had to have happened immediately *prior to* your achieving that completion. Before that? Before that? Keep imagining the steps until you get to the present moment, here in the room. (If you are working with a partner, he or she writes down your steps.) _____

  _____

  _____

  _____

- What would be your first step tonight? Tomorrow? This week? Are you willing to do that? _____

  _____

  _____

- How do you feel now? _____

  _____

  _____

- Write down only one step here and a specific date when you can move on it. Do not write down more than one step because you may not know what the second step is until you take the first one!

  _____

  _____

✔ In the next seventy-two hours, an answer or help will come to you. Avoid sharing your process with anyone who is overly skeptical or negative.

TIP CARD: All I have to do is what I love to do and am good at, which is _____

_____

_____

_____

_____

WHAT AM I LOOKING FOR?
FIVE-MINUTE WRITING EXERCISE

Studies have shown that simply acknowledging, identifying, and writing about our feelings concerning unemployment, loss of a relationship, or any other difficulty can release energy that, if kept in our body, could create blocks for future well-being and even prosperity. Therefore, begin to sift, sort, and generally turn over the soil of your inner ground of being. This should be done in a spirit of play, not work! You can use the following exercise anytime you want to move in a new direction.

What you need: kitchen timer or watch, notebook and pen or pencil, this workbook, a quiet place or table in a nice café, about fifteen minutes or less.

✔ Set a kitchen timer or your watch for five minutes. Start writing a stream-of-consciousness account of what you want to have in

---

SEVEN POINTS TO REMEMBER
WHEN TAKING A STAND

- *Anything is possible.* What you have done up till now need not limit where you are going.
- *You cocreate your world with universal intelligence and collective wisdom.* The more we ask for support—and we must ask—the more amazing coincidences begin to happen.
- *What you experience as the world—material reality—is but one aspect of a whole system of energy fields.* We have guardian angels, old friends, and groups of souls in the spiritual dimension who help us remember who we are and what we came to do.
- *You are always connected to this invisible world.*
- *You can make a difference in the quality of life.* Each individual purpose is essential to the whole.
- *Doing what matters is spirituality—integrity—in action.* When our goal is to be in integrity, we are already fulfilling our life purpose.
- *Fulfilling your life purpose contributes to the whole field and adds your weight to the critical mass.*

—Adapted from *The Purpose of your Life*[3]

your life at the moment. Where do you want to go? What do you want to feel like? What do you need? Write down anything that comes to mind. Keep your pen moving, and don't stop to think too much.

✔ Stop as soon as the timer rings.

✔ Review your writing, and circle the three words that are most highly charged to you.

✔ Underline one or two sentences that clearly say what you are looking for.

✔ Transfer the one or two sentences to your profile sheet, page 231, and date the entry.

✔ Transfer the three words to the profile sheet, page 231.

TIP CARD: I am looking for _____

_____

_____

_____

> **VISUALIZING PRACTICE**
>
> "The more you can actually experience the feeling of using a talent, the more you will attract opportunities for its expression. In addition to reading your working purpose statement each day, try this short, easy imagination practice:
> Think of one thing you love and do well. Close your eyes and remember the last time you did it. Really bring that positive feeling into your body through your imagination. Do this every day for three weeks. As soon as you are able to easily reconnect to that wonderful experience, you will begin to have requests for this talent or you will receive money for it."
> —*The Purpose of Your Life*[4]

WHAT I THINK STOPS ME FROM HAVING WHAT I WANT: FIVE-MINUTE WRITING EXERCISE

✔ Set your timer again. Start writing stream-of-consciousness style about what you think are the reasons you don't have what you want.

✔ Stop as soon as the timer rings.

✔ Review your writing and circle the three words that are most highly charged to you.

✔ Select one of the three words and begin your next paragraph with that one word. Include the other two words somewhere in the rest of the paragraph.

✔ Starting with your selected word, write about *how you would feel if you had what you wanted right now*. What would it feel like, smell like, look like, and sound like?

✔ Review your writing and underline your favorite sentence.

Anything Is Possible

Do you have a problem with the idea that anything is possible? What feelings arise when you read that statement?

- Write out any objections, arguments, or "proof" to the contrary.

  _____

  _____

  _____

  _____

- Where did you get your skepticism?

  _____

  _____

- Why do you choose not to believe anything is possible?

  _____

  _____

- Can you agree that you don't know what might happen tomorrow? Can you believe that there is an intelligence greater than yours at work in your life? _____

  _____

We live in a world of possibilities.

TIP CARD: *The obstacle I see is not the real issue. Anything is possible.*

WHAT TO DO IN THE MIDDLE OF THE NIGHT WHEN YOU ARE ANXIOUS

Keep this workbook or your journal close at hand. When you can't sleep, jot down any persistent thoughts to clear them out of your head. Let them go.

If you are feeling fearful about something, begin repeating a prayer of gratitude: "Thank you for all that I have received. Thank you for [specific things like good health, family members, friends, your house, your work]." The vibration of gratitude is a powerful healer and energy releaser.

Try not to "figure out" anything. Remind yourself that everything that has happened and is happening is strengthening you and is somehow necessary for you to learn, accept, or change. Notice who pops into your mind in a quiet way. How might this person have a piece of wisdom for you?

As you lie in the dark, send out loving energy to all the people who might be thinking of you or remembering you— all the people who saw you during the day, who have ever met you, and who may meet you in the future.

If you are lying awake because of anxiety about a meeting or task ahead of you, imagine yourself in the scenario. Fill your scene with pink radiant light, and imagine light in every corner. See yourself succeeding and receiving the rewards and results you so richly deserve. Notice that everyone is receiving his or her highest good at that moment as well. Thank God and All That Is for helping you accomplish all tasks with effortless ease. Let it go and go back to sleep. Tell yourself, all is well.

CULTIVATE SUPPORTIVE RELATIONSHIPS

> "At that time, my experience of spirituality and meditation seemed outside of the mundane life—too exalted. I gradually discovered for myself that the path in the world is the path to God. Living an ordinary life is the path to self-discovery. . . .
>
> [After a breakdown], I spent a number of years feeling adrift and confused. I did not try to control this chaotic time. I allowed it to teach me, and I desired to learn whatever lessons it brought. I knew that it was my process of individuation. During this period of not knowing what to do, I began to see the confusion as a good thing—as positive. I began to feel more empowered by living with not knowing than by a false certainty. . . .
>
> The ritual was very simple. . . . I just told myself to see through my everyday experiences. Just to take a look at what's going on . . . until we see the beauty in every ordinary experience . . . we see nothing. The secret of life is in seeing every tiny experience as a gift."
> —Brendan F.,
> in *The Purpose of Your Life*[5]

In the morning before you arise, remember to say, "Today I want to meet good people." During the day, look for people who seem to be on your wavelength. As you use your affirmation to attract new people with whom you resonate, take time to get to know them, invite them for tea or a walk. Begin to spend less time with people who continually drain your energy. In the new millennium, it will be critical to have built good, reciprocal relationships with a broad range of positive people. A sense of community enhances our lives spiritually, physically, and emotionally in subtle but profound ways. In the United States we must begin to reach out to others and remember the benefits of feeling part of an extended family, a neighborhood, and the larger community. Make your own family! Good relationships lead to feelings of support, relief, self-esteem, and security. A simple thing like bringing an apple-picking tool over to your neighbor for her apple tree and baking an apple pie with the apples can bring shared meaning and fun in a simple way that often gets lost in our dependence on sophisticated, expensive entertainment.

Think in terms of tribal support, and you can find many ways to be of service and participate in your life without changing the "big" things, like location, job, or schooling.

PART TWO

QUESTIONS
AND ANSWERS

CHAPTER 6

Ten Commonly Asked Questions About Finding Right Livelihood

⌘

Our relationship to time is what it is because we lie to ourselves about what we are and what we can do and we hide from ourselves what we are meant to be and what we are meant to serve.

—JACOB NEEDLEMAN[1]

If you are feeling confused and don't know how to start changing your life, you are not alone! Remember, your mind is going to insist that there must be one answer that will solve your dilemma. Your rational thinking process will demand that you make no moves until you have a definitive plan for moving ahead. In fact, life purpose *unfolds,* and the decisions you need to make get made in the moment they need to be made.

Take a moment to close your eyes and tune into that urgent, demanding, critical—even aggressive—voice that thinks you should get it together and *do it now.* Notice where this voice is located in your body. Is it in the tight cords of your neck? The circular thought patterns in your brain? The grinding of your jaw? The stab of pain behind the shoulder blades? The knot in your stomach?

If you can locate the place where you hold this tension, begin to send healing light into that spot. If you cannot find one spot in your body, simply focus on your breath, and imagine each breath carrying energizing light to all the cells of your body. Relax. Let go of the need to figure everything out. Your life purpose is safely perking away within you right now. You need not struggle. Let go of the need to do something, to go anywhere, to be different. Just relax. Keep breathing into your body. Whenever you're ready, open your eyes. Read through the questions that follow, and see if any apply to you. Then turn to the page noted and simply read with an open mind. Your own answers may suddenly become clear to you.

1. What if I don't know what my passion is? (below)
2. How do I transition out of a job where I have a secure paycheck into my own business? (page 83)
3. What if my new business doesn't seem to be getting off the ground? (page 88)
4. How do I define a new career when I don't know what I want? (page 89)
5. If I have artistic talent, how do I make that talent support me? (page 90)
6. What if I think I'm too old to start over? (page 92)
7. What if my partner is skeptical or not encouraging about my goals? (page 93)
8. Should I go back to school? (page 94)
9. Should I have a plan or just follow what life gives me? (page 95)
10. How can I balance career, marriage, and family? (page 97)

Question 1: What If I Don't Know What My Passion Is?

Think of your passion as something you cannot refrain from doing—something you do whether you get paid for it or not. Your passion is present in those moments when you are absorbed in a task and forget time. Your passion is present in your natural tendencies and your conscious interests.

In a spirit of fun and relaxation, answer the following questions, preferably in the company of good friends. Having fun with friends so often stimulates "off-the-wall" comments that hold surprising germs of truth!

✔ What do you feel most at home doing? (Do not count watching television.) Hints: getting together with friends, fixing something, gardening, giving advice, reading or studying, exchanging ideas, making plans, responding to a crisis, exploring, leading, taking risks, making sure things get done, teaching, healing, one-on-one interactions, group facilitation, giving hope, building a business. Summarize your answer on the profile sheet, page 232. _____
_____
_____

✔ List the activities you have done that you were so absorbed in you lost track of time. Summarize your answer on the profile sheet, page 232._____

_____

_____

✔ Whom do you admire? Why? Who has had a profound effect on your life? _____

_____

_____

✔ If a fairy godmother dropped in to grant you the ability to achieve a goal, and you knew you could not fail, what would you want to do? Summarize your answer on the profile sheet, page 232._____

_____

_____

_____

Question 2: How Do I Make a Transition out of a Job Where I Have a Secure Paycheck into My Own Business?

There is no one right answer for everyone. However, the following suggestions may help you clarify what is necessary or appropriate for your own situation.

Spiritual Perspective: Find the Purpose for Being at Your Present Occupation

✔ *Get clear about why you are working there.* The most important thing you can do to help release yourself from your present occupation is to get clear about what you came there to learn. For example, have you outgrown the growth challenges there? Have you learned to stand up for yourself? Have you learned to work with difficult people and not lose your equanimity? Have you acquired a skill? Are you truly finished with the job or just feeling a desire to run away? If the latter, you may well attract other, similar situations until you learn that lesson. Usually, the moment we have completed the task inherent in the situation (generally, a personal growth issue such as learning to set priorities, not undervaluing our worth, learning to listen, or realizing we cannot control others), something happens to move us out of that situation effortlessly (the company downsizes, folds, or moves, or our department demateri-alizes!).

✔ The most positive purpose I can see for being in this situation is

_____

_____

_____

✔ List everything you dislike about your present job, and explain why it is so important to you to find another kind or place of employment.

_____

_____

_____

✔ How is this job out of alignment with your values, or what you hold most sacred? Describe how it feels to be out of integrity. Summarize your answer on the profile sheet, page 232._____

_____

_____

_____

Mental and Emotional Preparations

✔ *Feel the feelings of leaving your old position.* Feel the fear of leaving the known and going into the unknown. Allow yourself to experi-ence the pain and the joy of growth.

✔ *Describe clearly what kind of situation will make you happiest.* What would make me happiest is _____

_____

_____

_____

Summarize your answer on your profile sheet, page 232.

✔ *Have patience.* Don't get discouraged because things don't happen as quickly as you would like.

✔ *Enjoy each step you take.*

✔ *Be prepared to grapple with personal issues as soon as you make your intention to move forward.* Whatever is your next growth step will pop up, even though it may look completely unrelated to your pro-fessional decision. You may have to improve your ability for tracking your finances, become a better multitasker, improve your public speaking, or become more decisive or assertive.

✔ *Don't burn bridges.* Freelance for your old employer for a while. Keep your transition clean. Leave with honor.

Physical Actions

✔ *Negotiate your time to work fewer hours.* Open up some quality time to do what you want to do part-time. State this intention clearly to yourself every morning (e.g., "I have five hours a week to find and work with new clients for my own business").

✔ *Set a date to leave that works for you and your boss.* Line up a couple of clients ahead of time.

✔ *Take one small step every day or week in the direction you want to go.* You'll be amazed at the synchronicities that draw good people and opportunities to you. For example, one woman turned her office manager skills into assisting one-person businesses until she could build her counseling practice. The step I feel like taking now is

_____

_____

✔ *Weed out clutter* at home and in the office.

✔ *Never sit with your back to your office door.* This principle of *feng shui* (the ancient Chinese system of harmonizing energy flow for success) is mandatory for maintaining positive energy flow.

✔ *Begin to complete unfinished projects.* The things I need to complete are _____

_____

_____

✔ *The first year of a transition can be difficult because you're dealing with a lot of unknowns.* That doesn't mean you've made a mistake. Keep your focus on what you want.

✔ *You are in a process. There is no end result.*

✔ *Have fun things to look forward to.* Don't be all work and no play because you feel scared about finances. Just for fun, I want to

_____

_____

_____

✔ *Be prepared to jump when the door opens.*

Relationship Support During Career Transition

✔ *Discuss your plans with your mate.* Express clearly and without guilt your need for a change. Come up with a workable plan together. If your mate resists your plans, go for short-term counseling to explore the issues. Don't give up on what you need just to placate your mate. Don't make everything black and white. Get creative about how you can make your transition without letting fear stop the process.

✔ *Tell your friends about your decision.* Choose a pal to be accountable to each week about the steps you plan to take. Do not share your plans with negative people.

✔ *Ask friends to refer clients to you.* The friends who come to mind are

_____

_____

✔ *Find other people who have moved in new directions and ask them what they did.* One woman, a lawyer who did litigation in a big firm, created her own small law office helping people collect their social security benefits. Instead of practicing a combative form of law that was hard on her health, she went back to her original calling, which was to help people. One person I admire is _____

_____

✔ *Partner with someone if it makes sense.* Be willing to change that decision if things don't work out, or if the person you have picked is extremely negative in his or her thinking. Be willing to cut your losses.

✔ *Join networking groups.* It's essential that you widen your contacts during the initial phases of building a business. Tell yourself every little step you take is getting you closer to your goal. The networking group I'm going to call today is _____

_____

_____

✔ *Be prepared to lose friends or acquaintances as you move forward.* Your courageous move may frighten others into looking at their own fears about moving on. Usually these are people with whom you have shared a "victim" mentality. Once you are no longer playing the "misery loves company" game, the basis of your friendship may change.

Financial Preparations

✔ *Make a simple business plan.* Have someone help you if you're not good at this. How much money do you need to make each month? How many clients do you need at what price per client? How much savings could you use each month to augment any shortfall?

✔ *Downscale expenses.* Simplify. Don't try to do everything when you are under the stress of a transition. I could let go of _____

_____

_____

✔ *Build savings.* You'll feel a lot less fearful if you have a savings account. What's your comfort level? Having two, three, six, twelve months of living expenses in the bank? Don't set such a high goal, however, that you never make the plunge! My goal is to save

_____

If You Have Serious Doubts
About Starting Your Own Business

✔ *Know yourself.* If you cannot face life without the security of a paycheck and the benefits of a job, don't try to be something you aren't.

✔ *Start slow, but be persistent.* If you want to build up a new multilevel sales business, no matter how exciting you feel it is, don't freak yourself out by trying to live on slow-building sales. Keep your day job, and build your clientele over time. If you have always been an administrative employee, it takes time to build your confidence in your salesmanship. However, set a time limit to leave your job, or a dollar amount in sales. Otherwise, you may stay too dependent on your day job, dissipating energy from the new career.

✔ *Take a new attitude at your place of employment.* In what way can you bring new life and pizzazz to your current situation? How would an attitude shift change your life where you work? Can you be even more fabulous an employee than you currently are? "If I stay in this job, I'm willing to _____

_____

✔ *Improve yourself.* Go to night school to increase your skills or develop an interest even if it doesn't look like a route to a paying job. Feeling good about yourself creates an attitude that attracts opportunities when you least expect them. Whenever you are learning something new, you are on purpose!

Question 3: What If My New Business Doesn't Seem to Be Getting Off the Ground?

✔ *If you are experiencing delays,* check your timing (see pages 143–144 in Chapter 9 for your Personal Year cycle). Be patient but give yourself a reasonable cutoff date by which time you will seriously consider stopping this line of endeavor and doing something else to bring in money.

✔ *If you are experiencing frustrations* (such as not attracting enough clients), answer these questions:

• What do I want? _____

_____

_____

• What's stopping me from having this? (Your answer will be a *belief* you hold about your ability to bring your goal to fruition.) _____

_____

_____

• What attitude, behavior, or expectation do I need to change? _____

_____

_____

• Is there anything I am afraid of happening if I were to succeed?

_____

_____

• Is there *any* emotional issue in my life that has not been fully resolved? _____

_____

_____

✔ Jot down any of your insights from this section that energized you even a little bit on pages 232–233 of your profile sheet.

Case History About Timing

Mary Patric (see her story on pages 148–151 of *The Purpose of Your Life*) worked at a job she hated. She was passionate about starting her own counseling business, but it wasn't going forward strongly enough to support her and her young daughter. After much anguish and frustration, Mary made the decision to let go of her dream for the time being. Instead, she decided to "turn toward" the job she hated so much. She shifted her attitude, saying, "Well, if I have to be here, I may as well make the best of it, and do the best job I can." Within three weeks, a new position opened up that allowed her to express her leadership; she got a company car, tripled her income, and began to enjoy the people in her new department. She concluded, "You don't have to find your

> "We live our lives—we think, feel and act—on the surface of ourselves, on the surface of an immensity that, were we to experience it, would answer all our questions and purify all the suffering of our lives. This immensity has many names. But we can call it the *Self*."
> —Jacob Needleman[2]

soul's purpose to find soul in what you are doing." Three years later, Mary left her employment on good terms with everyone, and she is now happily married and joyfully self-employed doing market research. "I know now that not being able to go forward in that other business was the best thing to happen. I see now I really didn't have the internal structure and life experience that a counseling career would have demanded. I love this business that I have created and the chance I have to stay home with my daughter!"

Question 4: How Do I Define a New Career When I Don't Know What I Want?

- Start with defining what you enjoy doing the most.
- Define the changes in your life that you want to make.
- Write down everything that catches your interest for one month.
- Commit to the idea that you want to work with people, things, ideas, and services that are really interesting to you. Find a way to receive some form of payment for your services.
- Don't consider careers that go against your philosophy, values, or interests.
- Apprentice yourself or volunteer for a short period, but don't give your services away if that doesn't feel reciprocal enough (i.e., you might be learning so much that it's worth it to work for free, but treat your time as valuable).
- Have a brainstorming session. Ask friends what they think your strengths are. NOTE: Do not invite people who are negative thinkers or who have an interest in your remaining in your niche.

- Put yourself "on assignment" to meet someone who will give you an idea about a new direction. Each morning before you get out of bed, affirm out loud, "Today I want to meet good people." (Refer to the Master Attracting Meditation on pages 111–112.)
- Find an unmet need near you. What needs doing in your area? Remember Helen K. Johnson's story in *The Purpose of Your Life*? She founded the reentry program for returning students at the University of California, Berkeley, because she herself was a returning student and saw a need to be filled for others like herself.
- Read inspirational books. Keep your intention strong to be shown your path.
- Take classes in any subject that interests you. Talk to the teachers and other students.
- Talk to people. Ask them if they know of any businesses or services that are exciting.
- Read the rest of this book. Take notes. Stay open and keep your attention on what you want. Relax. Find ways to have more fun — and then even more fun.

Jot down any of your insights from this section that energized you even a little bit on page 233 of your profile sheet.

Question 5: If I Have Artistic Talent, How Do I Make That Talent Support Me?

Writers write. Artists draw, paint, or sculpt. Designers draw floor plans and logos on cocktail napkins. Actors audition. They cannot help but do these things. If the drive to express is strong, you will find some way to receive money for what you do best. Life is not a sure thing. Your life purpose may require you to struggle in the backstages of life until you learn determination, humility, the illusion of glamour, or mastery of jealousy. If your creativity isn't supporting you, keep expressing it anyway and get a day job. Giving your time to painting, drawing cartoons, music, or theater is intrinsically rewarding. If it isn't, rethink your priorities and let go of the illusion. It's okay to let go of something that has died. On the other hand, try to introduce your natural talent everywhere even if you do it for free. Steve Bhaerman, whose stage name is Swami Beyondananda, began publishing a tiny newsletter featuring all his coworkers in a tree-trimming department in Michigan. The good-natured ribbing dished out to everybody from the top down not only defused some of the hierarchical tensions, but elevated the working atmosphere in general, encouraging some of the people to go on and reach their cherished goals beyond that job.

Master gem cutter Glenn Lehrer, who sold encyclopedias in the early days of his career, said, "All these years, I just pursued what I wanted to do because I love it. Now my industry is recognizing my work and seeing in it a major trend for the entire industry. I guess that's when you really know you are doing your life purpose. I've always thought, 'When you can't see the light [or the purpose], you go out and do what makes you happy. You won't be good for anybody anyway if you don't make yourself happy.' . . . Don't worry about what you can do with it, or if it will make money. Follow the passion. See where it takes you. . . . Your life has its own energy for seeking a state of perfection. You can never reach it, but something in your DNA seeks its highest state of existence. That is a law of nature."[4]

> "*Time rushes by because we are not engaged enough in life.* Not enough of our being is involved in our own life. To be devoured by our life is not to be engaged in living. On the contrary, when we are devoured by life it means the Self, one's own Self, is not present."
> —Jacob Needleman[3]

- Find a way to pay the rent.
- Do your art with gusto.
- Enjoy life to the fullest.
- Tithe 10 percent of your income.
- Take your art to those who don't have much beauty in their lives.
- Drop "poor me" language and take responsibility for coming into life as an artist.
- When choosing to make a career change to do your art, remember other times when you started out on a shoestring but built your finances up because you persevered. In the same spirit, be willing to start small, but be firm that your goal is to keep building toward job fulfillment with financial abundance. Avoid falling into the trap of either-or thinking ("either I'm happy with my job, and poor, or I hate my job, but I'm making a lot of money"). Anything is possible. Even *you* deserve to be happy!

Jot down any of your insights from this section that energized you even a little bit on page 233 of your profile sheet, or make yourself a TIP CARD.

Question 6: What If I Think I'm Too Old to Start Over?

So often we think: "If only things were different." We feel intimidated by the need to adapt to changing conditions, so we blame something outside ourselves. Excuses provide a convenient way to die without leaving the body. What else have you got to do with your time that's more fun than learning? If you're fifty and think, "If only I were twenty-five again!" think of it this way: You are twenty-five the second time around with all the knowledge you could have used then! Go ahead and answer the questions below that interest you the most.

✔ If money or age were no obstacle, what would make you leap out of bed in the morning, raring to go to your office, workbench, classroom, garden, or study? _____

_____

✔ What matters to you? How can you foster that in the world? _____

_____

_____

✔ How could you get a little bit of that into your life right now? Next week? _____

_____

_____

_____

✔ What older person is a role model for you? _____

_____

✔ What aspects of this person stand out for you?
   1. _____
   2. _____
   3. _____

✔ In what ways can you recognize those same aspects in yourself?
   1. _____
   2. _____
   3. _____

✔ Jot down any of your insights from this section that energized you even a little bit on page 233 of your profile sheet.

Question 7: What If My Partner Is Skeptical or Not Encouraging About My Goals?

When you experience any kind of major change in your life, such as a career move, a child leaving home, or remodeling your house, your vulnerability and sensitivity to everything automatically rises. If you are a person who is particularly oriented toward feeling guilty for rocking the boat, who tries hard to please everyone and keep the peace, making a job change could be disruptive to your family dynamics. The unspoken censure emanating from your partner could even derail you from your intention to find something more suited to your desires and needs. Review the following suggested affirmations and check the ones you need to remember the most!

- I need to listen carefully to the voice that tells me I need to make a change.
- I have a supportive group of friends who encourage me and help me keep on track.
- I don't let minor frustrations distract me.
- I don't fight other people's battles; I keep my energy for my own work during this transition.
- I know that these times of transition are necessary and precious.
- I keep things simple.
- I reassure my partner frequently that I love him or her and that my need to move forward is personal and not about him or her.
- I realize that my soul's need to develop is bigger than both me and my partner.
- I realize that something in me has shifted, and I need a different field of expression and a different way to serve others.
- I realize I may have to go over this ground with my spouse several times as I move forward.
- I make sure to have frequent, quality communication with my mate without feeling guilty for my needs or trying to appease him or her while neglecting what is true for me.

✔ Jot down any of the suggestions from this section that energized you even a little bit on pages 233–234 of your profile sheet.

Question 8: *Should I Go Back to School?*

If you have a persistent intuition that tells you to go back to school, listen to that voice. But if you feel ambivalent about that decision, you might want to ask yourself, "Is going back to school a way to hide out from life? Is it stalling? Does it support something I really love? Do I believe that the only way to get where I need to go is with this degree?"

Do you have any role models of people who are doing what they love and who don't have the so-called necessary degree? Is there another way to get where you want to go without the rigors of an educational program that you're not excited about attending? Is the degree important to you only to allow you to feel more credible?

Helen K. Johnson, founder of the reentry program on the campus of the University of California, Berkeley, faced the same fears and challenges of most returning students. Her advice? Find your own answers by writing a quick note addressing the following concerns:

✔ How can you build up the confidence in yourself to take this important new step?
✔ Describe your fears or concerns here.

_____

_____

_____

✔ Talk to friends or friends of friends who have gone back to school. Visit the reentry program of a college you wish to attend, or another one, just to get a feel for what you are thinking about. If you don't know anyone who has taken this step, ask in your morning meditation to get the answers you need. Notice who shows up!
✔ Can you go to school without burning any bridges? How? Ask for support in being shown how to do this (e.g., keeping a part-time association at your present job). _____

_____

_____

✔ How willing are you to make some adjustments to your lifestyle even if this feels a little uncomfortable? Student life requires changes in schedule, financial commitments, time away from family, and so on. Remember, your lifestyle change won't last forever! Take small steps, one class at a time. _____

_____

_____

✔ Are you willing to be a learner all over again? _____

_____

✔ What important kinds of experience would you bring into the classroom? _____

_____

✔ Can you take constructive criticism without using it as an excuse to
quit the class if things get tough? _____

_____

✔ If degrees were not an issue, what kinds of classes would *really*
excite you? Transfer this answer to your profile sheet, page 234. _____

_____

✔ Can you remember to seek out other students to build a support
network that will help you when you need it? _____

_____

Question 9: Should I Have a Plan or Just Follow What Life Gives Me?

By all means have a plan, if you can see logical steps to your goal.
Whatever you accomplish on that plan will give you the skills and
experiences that effortlessly build confidence. However, the crucial
point is also to be *open* to what life pre-
sents. Expect providence. Think in
terms of *both/and*: Both a motivating
and energizing plan that takes you forward, and an openness to what may be
even better.

Many people ask, "But how do I know
when to follow a new path? Maybe it's
just getting me off track. How do I know
which way to go?"

If you aren't able to visualize a plan,
how about defining your dream? Imagine a life that makes sense to you.
Remember Kermit Heartsong's story in
The Purpose of Your Life? He established
a successful board game business that
brought children and their parents

> "The day was full of
> sunshine, and it was a
> luxury to walk in the midst
> of all this warm and colored
> light. The days of September
> are so rich that it seems
> natural to walk to the end of
> one's strength . . . we were
> in excellent spirits, had
> much conversation, for we
> were both old collectors
> who had never had
> opportunity before to show
> each other our cabinets, so
> that we could have filled
> with matter much longer
> days."
>
> —Ralph Waldo Emerson[5]

together in a fun learning experience. But he also dreams of another life for himself one day. "This [board game business] is the path I'm on right now . . . I remember that when I was in high school I had a dream. I had the idea for an inner-city boarding school that would teach kids not only the basics, but more. Teach them languages, art, music. . . . I want to get to them when they're young. I want to excite them to learn. I want to let them know somebody cares about them. . . . I think I'll probably wind up working with children someday."[6]

When new ideas, events, or opportunities come to us, we compare them to our statement of *what we really want*. This is also the time to develop an operating statement, such as "I am a person who is generally successful in everything I do. I trust myself to make the right decisions." Or the knowledge that "I'm a writer." If someone comes along who wants you to manage a chicken farm, you have to ask, does that fit in with my bottom line of who I am? (It may be that managing a chicken farm would give you more time or space so you could also do your writing. Who knows?) You know. It gets back to trusting your process, checking into your intuition over a period of time. You may find you like to get feedback from your oracles (dreams, tarot cards, runes, *I Ching*, journal writing), meditation, or simply hashing ideas over with compatible friends. Don't be so afraid of making a mistake or a "wrong move" that you are constantly second-guessing yourself. Play a little bit. Who says you can't repair sailboats for a year? Who says you can't be a bagger at Lucky's for six months?

✔ What innovative ideas have you had lately that excited you that you didn't act on? _____
_____
_____

✔ Why didn't you? What are the most exciting elements about these ideas? _____
_____
_____

✔ Imagine one other way you might have those exciting elements in your life? _____
_____
_____

Question 10: How Can I Balance Career, Marriage, and Family?

Flying home from Los Angeles to the San Francisco Bay area, I happened to sit next to Jane and Mark Miller. They were returning home after participating in a ten-mile triathlon that included bike riding, running, and swimming in the ocean. I was so impressed with the success of their partnership, I asked them if they would share their story. They graciously agreed.

JANE AND MARK'S STORY

In 1992 Mark Miller was president of a fifty-million-dollar corporation, father of two children, and in the middle of a divorce. A few months past his fortieth birthday, Mark had not adjusted well to the idea of divorce. "My soon-to-be ex-wife suggested I go to a ten-day Native American Sun Dance retreat in the high desert outside Los Angeles, California. That's where I met Jane. Before the ten days were over, we had agreed to get married."

CA: That's incredible that the two of you came together so quickly. How did you decide where to live since you were living in Southern California, and Jane was in Northern California?

MM: Anybody looking at us from the outside would have predicted Jane would move to Los Angeles because I had so much more established there than she did. I owned a home and a five-acre horse ranch with six horses. I had children and was president of a large company. But even though I had so much more in terms of material things to "give up," I looked around and said, "No, this is not what life is about."

I began to extricate myself. I sold my house, even though it was a depressed market, and I lost money. I sold my horses, and accelerated the divorce process. I gave notice at work. I walked into the owner's office with a letter of resignation in one hand and a job application in the other. He looked up in disbelief as I handed him my job application for a sales job in our San Francisco branch. I was serious. I took a straight commission job in an area that was completely unfamiliar to me, where I had no customers to start with. I had a negative net worth when I arrived at Jane's little house in Mill Valley. I started over again.

CA: Did you feel on purpose in your life before you met Jane?"

MM: No. I had gotten to a point where I was starting to look for something that had to be within me. Meeting Jane forced me to become aware of how I was going to have to let go of my former beliefs about what success is. I certainly had the accoutrements of happiness — the horse ranch, climbing the corporate ladder. The hardest part was admitting that all of that hadn't gotten me what I wanted. I had this incredible void. There was a tendency to say, "Well, if this isn't it, let me go find what *it* is and fill it." I began to see that what I was looking for wasn't going to be a *thing*.

Life purpose for me was about things I needed inside myself. The things I wanted were more intangible — like quiet, solitude, partnership, camaraderie, fun, play, and to a certain extent security. In contrast to, let's say, fancy cars. I'm not sure I've even defined a life purpose yet in the last six years. It's not an overnight process of letting go of the old way of doing things. Even now I'm only beginning to get glimpses of what activities might fill the sensation of accomplishment and purpose.

I think there are twenty-year cycles. The first twenty years is basically childhood; the second twenty years of adulthood is about finding what is my power, where to put my energy, how to live up to the goals my parents set for me. Then comes the realization that our aging parents are our last line of defense before our own death. You have to ask yourself, "Why go through all this?" Are we just like ants carrying their crumbs thinking they're important?

CA: How do you think about the purpose of living for the next few years?

MM: As I look at my own future, I see words like *writing, creating, inventing, teaching, sharing*. More altruism. More giving than taking. It's more of a process than one particular goal that I will one day have.

CA: How does your relationship with Jane support your own life purpose?

MM: In prior relationships, each of us had a role to fill that was oriented toward some externally defined goal. For better or worse, we played out those roles. The relationship was held together by the goal. The problem, of course, is there was always this external prodding to do more and hold up your end of the bargain. There is usually one who is making it work or not work.

My relationship with Jane is different because it doesn't even come from the same place. It comes from a place of really wanting her to have her freedom to be and to grow. My role isn't to make her something. Her job isn't to further my something. My role is to be there in loving support for where she's going. We've discovered that the more we allow the other person to grow, the more we grow towards each other. We don't have to prove something or get the okay from the other.

CA: So, Jane. Tell us about meeting Mark for the first time.

JM: I was living in Mill Valley in a little house. I had been involved with the Navajos for four years, learning their traditions. There are certain preparations you are supposed to do before participating in the Sun Dance ceremony. I had already done the Sun Dance, and I didn't think I would do it again. But while I was doing the Eagle Dancing, I had a strong desire to do the Sun Dance again. Usually the preparation is at least six months, but I did it all in one month and went to the same Sun Dance retreat where Mark went on his ex-wife's suggestion.

I saw him across a field. I thought, "I have to get to know this man." I went over to the tepee where he was standing holding a feather fan that he was thinking of buying. I introduced myself and said how beautiful the fan was and that I had a fan back at my tent he would probably love to see. It was a fan given to me two weeks before by a medicine man. Twelve feathers of a red-tailed hawk. He came by a day or so later, and I showed it to him. We talked, and then he left.

My girl friend and I went to the swimming pond, and I looked up and saw him just getting into the water. I just walked over to him and climbed up on his back. I put my cheek against his and it felt like all our cells lined up. I said to myself, "Who is this man? I wonder if he feels this way?" And then I thought, "I'm going to marry this man." I never thought I would get married. I never met anyone I wanted to marry. If there is such a thing as reincarnation, I feel like we made an agreement to meet in this life.

CA: Your story does have the feeling of fate about it. Six years later, how do you see your life with Mark? How do you keep the magic?

JM: One of the reasons our relationship really works is that we're very committed to "getting off it." We don't get invested in having to have our own way. We both see the damage and drain it takes to have your relationship or business be the place where you act out. As much as possible we define who's responsible for what. For example, I manage the home checking account, and Mark manages the business account. We talk about any expenditures we are going to make over $300 (the amount used to be $50). Each of us has discretionary money. We used to be more rigid, but we both seem to have an internal clock that keeps us from overspending. We also have a rule where we give the other person absolute veto power over anything. For example, we could be going to Canada for a wedding. If on the way to the airport I said I don't want to go, the car would stop. If I had an intuition that we shouldn't go, we'd abide by that feeling. One of us is not dominant. We both have that power. We don't have big arguments about work. We discuss everything, and nothing much builds up. The first year we were under more pressure and we fought a lot, but we don't fight anymore.

In the beginning we made rules. For example, we couldn't have a fight and say we're stepping out of the relationship. We had a master circle surrounding us, and we could do whatever we wanted *inside it*. That allowed us this freedom to work out our stuff without splitting from each other.

CA: I know you own some businesses. How do you find time to work and play together or separately?

JM: We own commercial laundries and a few ATM machines, which we both manage, and I manage our mail order lock business. I also have a massage practice. Mark is a business broker; he sells businesses. Our lives are full. I am deeply involved in a spiritual school called the Diamond Heart Training. I also like to exercise every day. I make quilts. I have my own friends, both male and female. Mark does photography, and he invents things. He has his own friends, too, and they happen to be mostly female! He also does horseback riding and studies Neurolinguistic Programming. We both love to ski, exercise, do races like the triathlon, and travel. We've studied *Tantra* (the practice of spiritual sexual union) together and also have a great sex life!

CA: It sounds like you are both on your own spiritual path.

MM: The outer manifestation of our inner spiritual beliefs is seen in our values. Our ways of looking at the world are identical. We will evaluate something at the same speed and come up with the same thought.

JM: Our main rule in business is integrity. We're very clear about morality. We're very clear about money and all our dealings. We have clear budgets and goals even though we have irregular income. When there is excess money, we discuss whether it's better to save, invest, or buy something we want.

We never try to convert each other. We have a lot of room to have our own thoughts about our soul. Mark's given me so much. For example, I didn't want to give birth, and he's provided me with his two children, whom I adore. We've had to work at our relationship every day. We do things together to keep the romance going.

PART THREE

GETTING FOCUSED

CHAPTER 7

"But What Do I *Do?*"

[The acorn theory] claims that each life is formed by its unique image, an image that is the essence of that life and calls it to a destiny. As the force of fate, this image acts as a personal daimon, an accompanying guide who remembers your calling. The daimon's "reminders" work in many ways. The daimon motivates. It protects. It invents and persists with stubborn fidelity. It resists compromising reasonableness and often forces deviance and oddity upon its keeper, especially when it is neglected or opposed. . . . It has affinities with myth, since it is itself a mythical being and thinks in mythical patterns.

—JAMES HILLMAN[1]

KEEP YOUR FOCUS ON WHAT YOU WANT

Do you feel that you don't even know what you want? This is common and understandable. Just consider for one moment how many times a day you are bombarded with advertising messages about products that you momentarily think about and either immediately reject, wish you had, or actually go out and buy. Your attention is continually being pulled by what other people want you to think about or do. Not only that, but you may have chosen life goals that were based on pleasing members of your family rather than on your own innate purpose and values. We are not often encouraged to think for ourselves or to venture far from the cultural norm. If you are unemployed, you may be feeling overwhelmed at the acceleration of changes in the workplace, discouraged by rejection, or absolutely clueless about how to make yourself useful to companies who may not even exist in a year. If you are working for a company where rumors of layoffs and mergers are rampant, how do you know what your future might bring? Uncertainty, fear of change, and a feeling of helplessness in the face of events outside your control naturally will upset your equilibrium if you do not have a daily centering practice to tune into your inner guidance.

When you decide to explore what would make you feel happy, ful-filled, secure, joyful, and confidently challenged, try to focus on the feeling that you ultimately want to experience. To make a statement of intent, you don't have to get stuck writing down all the specifics (unless you know for sure that you want to live in a log cabin in the northwest section of Vermont, writing crime novels and living with a mate who paints pictures of parrots and is five feet nine and one-half inches tall, and with a red Porsche parked in the garage and tickets to Tahiti tucked into your passport in the top left-hand drawer of your antique rolltop desk). Keep it simple. How do you want to feel? Keep your focus on being led to the perfect opportunities that allow you to be happy, to be of service in attunement with your abilities and desires, and to be well rewarded.

> "Studies of high-performing people in many fields show that successful, effective people tend to visualize the results they want in their lives and work, and to affirm to themselves that they will accomplish these goals. They create a clear and conscious intention to achieve certain outcomes and then allow that frequently affirmed intention to guide their actions. Rather than planning what they will do and how they will go about it, they start by creating an intensely alive mental representation of the end state. That representation then works through the individual's intuition and unconscious mental processes as he or she makes the multitude of everyday decisions that bring the goal ever nearer."
> —Willis Harman[2]

TURN YOUR QUESTION INTO RESULTS

What are you currently in a quandary about? What question, large or small, is on your mind right now (besides "What do I want for lunch?") Are you stewing about whether you should move to another city? Do you want to go back to school but don't know in what field? Are you wishing you could find another job? Are you thinking of doing network mar-keting? What is your current question? The process of turning your question into an affirmative statement of results is simple but profound. If used often, this process will attract things to you effort-lessly, but you have to have a vivid pic-ture and feeling connection to what it is that you are looking for.

To restate your current question as a

positive affirmation, first ask yourself why you are asking the question at all. For example, a young woman named Jill asks the question: "Should I marry Joe?" Why is she asking the question? Because she wants to know if Joe is the right person to marry. Underlying her question is the desire to be happily married. She's not sure if Joe is the right man for her. Jill can rewrite her question, "Should I marry Joe?" to express the results that she is looking for, such as "I am now happily married to the perfect person for me." Or perhaps, "I am a loving person who is deeply loved." That way, she reframes her confusion and question into a statement of the results she is looking for.

Software programmer Dennis P. asks this question: "Should I move to Colorado?" What he wants in his heart is to be closer to nature, continue his software programming without commuting, and be able to ski more often. But he's not sure his business will go well if he moves away. Dennis might rewrite his question thus: "I am living in a beautiful, serene atmosphere that increases my creativity and financial well-being so much that I can ski several times a winter."

The point is to ask yourself what you *really* want—bottom line—and then focus on that, *even though you may feel you don't have a clue about how that might come about.* Since we are cocreators with universal energy, opportunities will be made available for us, as long as we ask for support in a particular direction. It's *our* business to express the direction we'd most like to go in and let the universe "rearrange the furniture." Of course, the next step for us is to listen carefully to suggestions from our inner guidance, notice where our attention is drawn, follow through on synchronicities, and take action where we feel a strong pull of energy. Try it yourself.

MOVE FORWARD WITH INTENTION

- Write out your question.
- State what it is that you are looking for.
- Put that statement into present time (i.e., I now have or I am now . . .).
- Don't use any negatives as in "I now am rid of all the rotten people in my life." Instead, write something like "I have a wonderful circle of compatible friends."
- The statement should make you feel happy, energized, and opti-

mistic. Feeling a little tingle of excitement is a good sign you're connected to your purpose.
- Close your eyes and ask yourself:
     Do I feel that I really deserve this?
     Can I allow myself to be this happy and on purpose?
     Do I have any reservations about having this?

If you can feel in your body that you deserve what you desire, that you can allow it into your life, and that you have no reservations about having this much good fortune, then you are certain to achieve your affirmation soon. The time frame for receiving your results will depend on your inner beliefs about time and how long it takes to achieve results. If you are not too restricted in your beliefs, the speed of the results could astound you.

If, on the other hand, you feel a little ambivalent about deserving good fortune or don't know if you can allow this good fortune into your life, it's okay. Recognizing doubt is useful because then you can work with that awareness. If you have any reservations about what you are asking for, add a variation of the following to your affirmation: "this or something better." For example, a woman named Gloria said, "I am now working at home and earning a good living from my child care service or doing something that is even better for all concerned."

TWELVE SIMPLE WAYS TO START
THE WHEELS IN MOTION

A person I met the other day said, "I'm working in a bookstore in accounts receivable, and I'm clueless about how to pursue my life purpose. What do I do?" Here are some simple but profoundly helpful tips to follow when you feel clueless.

1. *Don't be downcast! Express gratitude.* Your present job is paying the bills so you can have time to ask the deeper questions in life! So far so good. Be grateful for what you have already achieved, and don't look down on it as "not enough" or "not right."

2. *Identify your strengths.* In what ways do you excel in your *present* job? _____

_____

_____

3. *Get real about your priorities.* You are not a victim of circumstance. Your past choices have resulted in the present situation. Why did you take this job over another one? Why was that important to you? Is it still important to you? _____

_____

_____

_____

4. *Face the truth.* In what ways have you outgrown this job or situation? _____

_____

_____

5. *Describe exactly how you'd feel if you were living your life purpose.* How would your life be different if you were on purpose?

_____

_____

_____

_____

6. *Describe who you are without talking about your present or past job titles.* What do people say you do in the world? What do people say about you? What's your best attribute whether or not you get paid for it? What do you do even without getting paid for it? Let the universe know that you are ready and willing to be used in the best possible way right now! What I love to do is _____

_____

_____

_____

Rewrite your answer about what you love to do on page 230 of the profile sheet.

7. *Notice what is coming into your field of vision or action.* What three things have caught your attention lately? _____

_____

_____

_____

Rewrite your answer about what's caught your attention lately on page 229 of the profile sheet.

8. *Take action.* Is there some way to follow up on the things that are attracting your attention? A class? A phone call to someone? What one step could you take this week toward something that you like to do?

_____

_____

9. *Explore something different from your routine.* Life is a journey, a process, and a day-by-day adventure. There is no end result. Answer the question, "How can I get more adventure into my life?"

_____

_____

_____

Record your answer on pages 234–235 of your profile sheet.

10. *Change your schedule.* Are there hours, afternoons, or weekends when you tend to do busywork or watch TV because you don't know what else to do? What activity could you put in that time slot that (1) is really fun, (2) is good for you, (3) is something you've been wanting to do, (4) is completely new for you, (5) will teach you something new?

_____

_____

11. *Set a clear intention that you want to meet good people to assist you in making your life more wonderful.* Each morning (1) give thanks for what you have, (2) ask for what you want, (3) assume your prayers are answered, (4) pay close attention to everything that happens next, and (5) do not fail to take action when you get a good feeling or straight-out intuitive idea.

12. *Repeat this process. Trust your process.* Notice where you are in six months!

WHAT TO DO NO MATTER WHAT

Put these suggestions on TIP CARDS to keep handy in times of stress.

- Simplify any way you can.
- Take care of yourself. Breathe. Get back into your body.
- Back off a little.
- Keep your focus on what you want.
- Assume there is a purpose to what's happening.
- Trust the process.

✔ Which of the preceding suggestions would make the biggest positive difference in your life? Make a note of this on page 235 of the profile sheet.

THIRTEEN PRINCIPLES TO HELP YOU STAY ON TRACK

I suggest that you write each of these principles on separate 3 × 5 index cards to keep with you or near your work area. Whenever you feel you need insight, pull one out. Even small reminders like this help keep us on track!

1. You were born for a purpose.
2. You are a magnetic field.
3. Anything is possible.
4. Stay in gratitude and positive energy.
5. Look for the meaning or purpose in what you are doing.
6. Participate more and plan less.
7. Start anywhere; purpose is not linear—it's surprising.
8. You don't have to become a different person.
9. Focus on what you want, not what you don't want.
10. Love what you do. Do what you love.
11. Pay attention.
12. Listen carefully to your intuition.
13. Take action on intuitions.

TIP CARDS: Write each one of these words on separate index cards and keep them in your wallet, pocket, or purse. Draw one each day to hold the focus: *Gratitude, Priorities, Strengths, Truth, Feelings, Passion, New Ideas, Action, Exploration, Change, Intention, Trust.*

MASTER ATTRACTING MEDITATION

Here is the intention exercise given to me by author and master teacher Giorgio Cerquetti, who spent many years studying Vedic philosophy and yoga in India. The author of *The Vegetarian Revolution* and *Incontro con la Chiara Luce* [Encounter with the Clear Light],

Giorgio told me, "This exercise is deceptively simple, but it combines all the yoga systems. Stillness comes from *hatha yoga* (physical postures). Breathing comes from *pranayama* (breathing exercises). The inner silent mental repetition is *dhyana yoga* (meditation yoga). The out-loud affirmation is *mantra yoga* (or repetition of a sacred sound)."

As soon as you begin to use this streamlined meditation, watch for the appearance of the very things you want, seemingly with little struggle or sense of effort. If practiced correctly and regularly, this meditation brings amazing results in a relatively short period of time. It works like clear water flushing through the pipes of your system to clear away nonuseful beliefs.

The key to this meditation is in reaching complete stillness before speaking your mantra. In this case, physical stillness provides a fertile receptivity, much like silence in a recording studio. With physical immobility, your unconscious is more sensitive to taking in and recording new messages that repattern your old operating beliefs. Remember when your teachers used to ask you to sit still? They wanted you to listen and take in information!

Following are six mantras (positive affirmations) for use with this meditation. Try to do each of them once a week, but make sure to do the First Awakening Mantra every morning for at least twenty-one days in a row (this saturates your unconscious with the new energy).

You may change the wording to suit your own style, but if you create your own affirmations, say exactly the same words each time you use them. For example, don't say "I love myself" one day and "I love myself very much" another day. To maintain consistency, it's a good idea to write out your affirmation so that you won't forget the exact wording.

It's fine to read the affirmation from your notes until you have the wording memorized. Write each affirmation on a 3 × 5 index card so that you can put it somewhere easy to retrieve when you are sitting still. Also, you might want to post your affirmation somewhere where you can see it frequently, for example, in your bedroom, car, or kitchen.

If you want to practice this meditation in a group, divide into partners, and try to keep the room fairly quiet as people say their mantras aloud to each other. Have one person read the affirmation word by word to a partner, who then repeats the mantra out loud while remaining completely still and focused. Then switch and let the other person do his or hers.

Positive Affirmations (Mantras)

1. Say this every day before arising from bed:
   "Today I want to meet good people."

2. *Self-esteem* (choose one or two):
   "I have within myself all the qualities and the resources to fulfill my needs and desires."
   "I authorize myself to accept the abundance and wealth I deserve."
   "I have the courage to know myself."

3. *Life purpose* (say both):
   "I love life."
   "I am ready to discover and enjoy the purpose of my life."

4. *Love* (say all four sentences):
   "I deserve a partner compatible with my sexuality, spirituality, and lifestyle."
   "I love myself."
   "I love others."
   "I allow others to love me."

5. *Health and well-being* (say all three; you can say these anytime during the day, also):
   "I am healthy, peaceful, and balanced." (NOTE: If you are ill and don't feel healthy, say, "I choose to be healthy, peaceful, and balanced" to reinforce your free will and desire for health.)
   "I send the people around me peace, love, and health. (This expands compassion.)
   "I deserve to be healthy, peaceful, and balanced." (This reduces and eliminates any guilt about deservingness.)

6. *Relationships and influence* (say both):
   "I send my love and good energy to all the people thinking of me, remembering me, and looking at me." (This is good for actors, models, and anyone working with an audience.)
   "I wish for all the people I have met in this life peace of mind, the best health, good fortune, and happiness."
   Now, try it! Choose the set of mantras you wish to start with.

How to Do the Meditation

1. *Asana, or sitting position. Take a comfortable position. Become still.* Find a position you can hold for five minutes without moving the feet, hands, shoulder, head, or fingers. You may lie down, but sitting is preferable in order to do the breathing exercises. If any part of the body moves, you are not in stillness.
2. *Breathing.* When you reach your still position, close your eyes. Take three soft, deep inhalations. *When you breathe in repeat mentally, "Energy in." When you breathe out, say mentally, "Problems out."* If you prefer, you may also say mentally, "Energy in, energy out." Do three full cycles. If you wish to do more, do seven full cycles, but three is enough.
3. *Focus.* Choose an object or spot on the wall in front of you on which to focus your eyes. After completing the three breathing cycles, *open your eyes without moving any other part of the body, and focus on your object or spot.* Keep your gaze straight on that object without moving. It's okay to blink, but don't move your gaze.
4. *Saying aloud the mantras you have chosen* and keeping the body still, *slowly repeat your positive affirmation aloud word by word.* Don't rush the process. Repeat three times.
5. *Final breathing.* When you finish saying the mantra, *close your eyes again. Remain still.* This time when you do the breathing, mentally say on the in-breath, "Love in," and on the out-breath, "Love out."

KIM'S STORY

Kim B., from South Africa, wrote a letter about the changes in her life following a decision to start reading "as much inspirational material as possible to help lift me up out of the doldrums." She had just finished reading *The Tenth Insight: Holding the Vision: An Experiential Guide.*

Five years ago I found out that my husband was having an affair. . . . I accepted this and thought that it was probably a midlife crisis where two people had become complacent, look for excitement, and that the novelty would eventually wear off. . . . [However,] after five years of this, I realized that I had become a very depressed person. . . . The whole situation came to a grinding halt when he suggested that we move to J. (600 km away) and start all over again. I came to a number of conclusions:

1. I attend a yoga class twice a week, and used this time to meditate on the problem. I asked for positive energy to replace negative thoughts and emotions. I asked for assistance from my spirit guides and God, and then let it go.
2. I realized that it was my husband's problem, not mine. I had offered as much assistance as possible without being judgmental.
3. I came to the conclusion that we have probably come full circle, and learned all we can from each other, and now have to move on.
4. I am fascinated by the mention in *The Tenth Insight* [by James Redfield] of animal spirits that affect our daily lives . . . the other day I was taken aback when I saw this enormous crow sitting on a fountain. I read in the book that the crow is the omen of change. I took the appearance of the crow as a sign that I am on the right path.
5. I listen to my intuition more often now, and share ideas with my colleague, C.; talking helps, and I don't feel so alone anymore.
6. My husband and I have . . . agreed to a trial separation. I will have the space and opportunity to develop myself without the stress of him and the other woman. Even she has decided to leave her husband and start off on her own. We are all moving once again.
7. I have a totally different attitude toward life and people. I realize that the more I am of service to other people, the less time I have to mope about my situation.
8. I make a point of giving thanks every day for everything I feel grateful for. Every time I have a negative thought, I ask for assistance to remove this way of thinking and focus on the positive aspects. I even relate better to my children; I listen to their problems without making it my problem and wanting to fix it for them.

9. Certain people who used to irritate me, no longer bother me. I realize that we are working together to clear past differences and look upon it as an opportunity to do so in this lifetime. . . .

10. I ask myself, 'Does this person have a message for me? What can I learn from them and how can I share this with others?' I remind myself that they also have a birth vision; I have learned to listen without passing judgment, and to overcome my fears."

✔ Circle one or two ideas that stood out for you in Kim's story. Record your insights on page 235 of your profile sheet.

CHAPTER 8

Writing a Working Purpose Statement

Every day I experience the benefits of peace of mind. It's very good for the body. As you might imagine, I am a rather busy man. I take many responsibilities upon myself, activities, trips, speeches. All that no doubt is a very heavy burden, and still I have the blood pressure of a baby. . . . Good food, a struggle against every excessive desire, daily meditation, all that can lead to peace of mind; and peace of mind is good for the body. Despite all the difficulties of life, of which I've had my share, we can all feel that effect.

—His Holiness, The Dalai Lama[1]

You are an organizing field of energy with an inherent purpose. Your purpose *is* working—emerging in the activities you choose, the way you see yourself, and through your values. Self-awareness is a process. Be patient, and take time to ask for guidance and look for confirmation and direction. If you still don't feel that your life is on track, perhaps writing a working purpose statement will help increase your awareness of how you contribute to the world. With any increase in awareness, our lives begin to take on more meaning and movement. Linda's story at the end of the chapter is a good example of how success follows positive inner changes.

You can do the following exercise by yourself, but it's much more fun to do with one or more good friends. Others see elements in you that may be hidden from your eyes.

HOW TO WRITE A WORKING PURPOSE STATEMENT

Step 1: *I Love to . . .*
Circle the words from the "Activities" box that follows that best represent you. Jot down any such words that apply to you but are not listed.

Look for things that are *absolutely easy* for you to do, things that you may not have received any training in but are just "good at." What do you have a knack for?

Transfer these descriptive words to your **working purpose statement** on pages 120–121.

ACTIVITIES

I LOVE TO:

talk	listen	teach	write	sew	tinker
garden	repair	analyze	drive	sail	walk
run	mentor	paint	read	beautify	win
surf	collect	persuade	explore	feed	cook
record	solve	negotiate	heal	support	reveal
edit	critique	direct	produce	campaign	inspire
advocate	clear away	guide	dance	research	bake
counsel	coach	build	invent	trouble-shoot	soothe
travel	lead	manage	correct	develop	measure
find	collaborate	challenge	overthrow	stare out the window	

Step 2: I Am . . .

Circle the qualities that you love about yourself in the "I Am" box. Include what others have said about you. Resist the temptation to be modest about your qualities, and don't be limited by this list. Write your qualities on your working purpose statement.

I AM:

humorous	enthusiastic	comforting	determined	intelligent
kind	courageous	direct	inspiring	supportive
visionary	compassionate	flexible	entertaining	knowledgeable
open	generous	strong	energetic	calm
persuasive	persevering	insightful	spontaneous	quick thinking
scholarly	careful	outgoing	musical	solitary
patient	pragmatic	artistic	discriminating	philosophical
gentle	optimistic	practical	adventurous	original
social	loyal			

Step 3: *I Would Like to Have More . . .*

Circle the qualities that you would *like* to possess from the following box, or write down other qualities that are not listed here. Write your qualities on your working purpose statement.

I WOULD LIKE TO HAVE MORE:

fun	capacity to love	ability to make people laugh
generosity	leadership ability	ability to bring peace
compassion	self-confidence	artistic or musical ability
kindness	inventiveness	capacity to heal
courage	spiritual clarity	capacity to rise to an occasion
faith	snazzy elegance	time to be of service
humility	dancing skill	trust during uncertainty
integrity	common sense	uncommon sense
creativity	ability to present complex material simply	positive impact on environment or human rights
tolerance		
fairness		

Step 4: *Recognizing and Remembering Myself*
Continue to answer questions 4 through 13 on the working purpose statement as quickly as you can, without thinking too much about each one. Let the answers flow without judgment.

WORKING PURPOSE STATEMENT

1. Activities I love to do are (see box, page 118) _____
   _____
   _____

2. I am (see box, page 119) _____
   _____
   _____

3. I'd like to have more (see box, page 119) _____
   _____
   _____

4. When I was a child, I wanted to be _____
   _____
   _____

5. When I was a child, I always loved to _____
   _____
   _____

6. What interested me *this morning* (or *this week*) was _____
   _____
   _____

7. How could this interest be related to my purpose at this time?
   _____
   _____
   _____

8. The qualities I like best about myself are _____
   _____
   _____

9. I shine when _____
   _____
   _____

10. I excel at _____
    _____
    _____

11. I am most myself when _____

_____

_____

12. What I do effortlessly is _____

_____

_____

13. I keep being drawn to _____

_____

_____

Step 5: I'm "in the Business of"

Maybe you'd like to get a cup of tea now and review the answers on your working purpose statement. Your next task is to take the raw data about yourself and combine it into one statement—to distill the essence of yourself into one short, snappy, imaginative purpose statement. Take your time combining all your elements. *To be a truly effective working purpose, this sentence must carry an emotional charge that either brings tears to your eyes or makes you laugh with delight!*

✔ I am "in the business" of _____

_____

_____

_____

✔ Write your new purpose statement on page 235 of your profile sheet.

EXAMPLES OF PURPOSE STATEMENTS

To give you the idea of what a purpose statement sounds like, here are some examples from students in our workshops:

Susan R. (an emergency physician who became a consultant and public speaker on natural health care reform and physician leadership): **"I am in the business of healing the healers."**

Cathy M. (former franchise business consultant): **"I'm in the business of storytelling."**

Anthony K. (recently retired): **"I'm in the business of starting over, and enjoying it!"**

Dick F. (recently retired): "**I'm rediscovering myself.**"

Liz P. (sales representative): "**I'm in the business of motivating and inspiring other people.**"

Sandra S. (accountant): "**My purpose is doing new age healing with animals.**"

Patricia D. (flight attendant, Herbalife distributor, and realtor, who now wants to connect with others): "**I'm in the business of doing creative work with my soul group.**"

Linda S. (executive assistant): "**I seem to be in the business of using my intellect and creativity to make lives easier.**"

Sharon A.: "**I'm in the business of being knowledgeable and entertaining.**"

Victoria O.: "**I'm about nurturing and coaching myself and those around me to reach beyond—seeking alternative solutions within the context of teaching.**"

Bruce B. (multifaceted artist and children's storyteller): "**My purpose is the creation of brilliant new worlds.**"

Nancy M.: "**I solve challenges by organizing all the parts needed to manifest the result.**"

Ken H.: "**I gather and analyze natural health care information and disseminate it.**"

Andreas V. (a pilot who wanted more freedom in his life and who felt isolated by his work): "**My purpose now is to fly freely in a flock!**"

Don M. (a retired oil executive now drawn to develop his spirituality): "**I'm moving to higher ground.**"

Notice that most of these purpose statements are open-ended and broad-based. They allow people to stay in contact with what is vital to them, which will effortlessly attract specific tasks and opportunities. If God is looking for someone to do a certain job, make sure She knows who wants the assignment.

Linda S., an administrative assistant in a high-level recruiting organization, came to a workshop I gave in Los Angeles. She was so radiant and excited about her life, I felt drawn to talk to her about how her life had changed so dramatically in the past few months.

LINDA'S STORY

"My whole life has changed spectacularly in the last few months. A year ago I was having financial difficulties and was so depressed about my work. I was not at all respected or appreciated for what I was doing. It seemed like I had felt unappreciated all my life. I was working hard, but not getting anywhere. I've been a secretary since high school. I'm a good secretary, but that's all I had on my resume. I was so discouraged, I was ready to become a gardener.

"I saw the book *The Purpose of Your Life* on *Oprah*, and I immediately thought, 'I need that book.' I got the book, and started working on my mission statement. I realized that I have to be able to use my creativity—it just comes out through my fingertips. If I deny myself that creativity, it gets all backed up inside me, and I start running in circles. It has to come out. So my mission statement had to include using creativity. The other points about me are that I'm a great organizer, and I like to help people out. So I thought, 'You know what? I *am* in the right profession!' But I didn't want to sell myself out with just any job. I need to be with someone who respects me and appreciates me for what I'm good at. So the purpose statement got me refocused and clearer about what I needed to find and how I wanted to feel.

"I was working with the CEO of an Internet company, but they were going to relocate where I knew nobody, and I didn't want to leave my friends. So I knew I was going to lose my job, but how to find the right one? One of directors on the board of our company is a top Hollywood player, and I frequently dealt with his office. One day I was talking with his assistant, and I asked her how she got her job, and she said, 'I had no intention of working when I came to Los Angeles, but a recruiter got my résumé and found this job for me in three days.' That got my attention, so I asked her for the recruiter's name! I called the recruiter, and within two weeks I got this fantastic job. I work for executive recruiters, and this job fulfills everything on my mission statement. We help people find jobs all over the world, so it is far beyond the normal realm of just helping your immediate team. I'm helping a whole network of people and being able to see the results of my work.

"My new boss totally supports and backs me up. Not even my parents did that. That feeling of support makes me grow, which makes me more creative naturally. I'm making twice my old salary. For the first time in my life, I feel like I'm getting paid what I'm worth. When I was young, I was always criticized for not getting along well with others, because I am so independent. Now, for the first time, I'm working with a group of people who all get along. There's no friction or politics. It's like a family. It's amazing.

"It blows me away that changing little things and looking at things differently would change so much. A friend says that my laugh even sounds better."

What made the difference for Linda?

"It was sitting down and stating what I'm good at, and recognizing that for myself. What am I truly? I had never really acknowledged my strengths before. I believe that is what got me the right placement. What is so fascinating to me is that I stayed true to myself, even though I was in a financial crunch. But because *I* was able to recognize my own value, I was able to attract others who would reward me for it.

"It's funny, but now I'm a role model for others in transition. They come to me, and I tell them, 'Be true to yourself.' One of my good friends just changed to a super job, and she is so happy. She saw what I did and saw she could do it too. It's a trickle-down effect.

"Another important lesson for me was to see the purpose behind everything that happens as important information that could indicate what new direction to take. For example, I was sitting around every weekend trying to rent my condo. Nobody was coming, and I resented it as a big waste of time. Finally, I decided to show it from two to four only, take it or leave it. I rented it the very next day. I recognized that my feeling of resentment about wasting time sitting around was a signal for me to change my tactics. If it wasn't working, okay, change something. And I did. And it worked. I'm learning to work with situations, relax, and let it happen."

✔ What touched you most about Linda's story? Make a note of that on page 235 of the profile sheet. _____

_____

_____

_____

CHAPTER 9

Tracking Relevant Information

∽

Reading the book of nature, becoming acquainted with nature's patterns by watching the sun, the moon, and the stars, can educate a person in the mysteries of the body and soul. The byproduct of this kind of education of the heart is a life full of warmth, charm, and meaning.

—THOMAS MOORE[1]

STRENGTHEN YOUR INTUITIVE LISTENING

If our life purpose is inherent, the way we hear its guidance is to listen with our inner ear, or intuition. Generally, we try to figure things out with our mental processes of deduction and our analysis of past experience, guided by our desire to control the future. Intuition is a direct message that most often comes to us in quiet moments, but it can also jolt us into action in the thick of tumult. To clarify what is meant by intuition, let's review some of the most often asked questions about it.

What does intuitive mean?

The *Random House Dictionary* defines *intuition* as "direct perception of truth, fact, etc., independent of any reasoning process; immediate apprehension; a keen and quick insight; pure, untaught knowledge." Intuition is having a thought or insight enter your mind directly without going through a logical, factual explanation process. It presents an idea for the next step in your life, or it may give an answer to a question you have been holding in your mind but have forgotten about for a while. Intuition is also involved in those first impressions you pick up when meeting someone new.

Is intuition like hearing a voice?

Intuition is a subtle form of communication that is experienced directly as a thought in the mind, a prickly feeling on the skin, an inner uneasiness, a feeling of *yes!*, an inner voice, or even a vision. Nancy Rosanoff, author of *Intuition Workout*, says, "There are three primary ways in which intuition speaks to us: through images and symbols [mental], through feelings and emotions [emotional], and through physical sensations [kinesthetic]."[2] For example, you may have a direct *mental* thought come into your mind such as "I need to go back to school." The thought persists. You suddenly notice other people talking about their educational experiences. You see notices on bulletin boards for scholarships. There's a college catalog left on the only available table in a café. Your mind keeps returning to the idea of school.

In another scenario, a young man wakes up early and feels restless. He tries to work but can't keep his concentration. He suddenly remembers he didn't call his mother last weekend because friends dropped by. He wonders if he should drop his car off for an oil change in the morning. He fidgets all morning, talking on the phone, feeling unsettled. Later that afternoon he gets word that his father had a heart attack earlier that day while driving to the grocery store. His intuition was sending *emotional* warning signals all day, but he didn't tune in carefully to what he was feeling.

In a third case, a woman walks into a room and hears a stranger talking to someone. Hearing the stranger's voice sends chills through her body and raises the hair on her arm. She thinks, "That voice. Where is this person? I want to meet the person who is speaking." People who are "kinesthetic" types frequently experience intuition somatically.

How do I know it's my intuition talking to me and not my fears or my ego?

Intuition is usually persistent but without a sense of urgency. Of course, if you are in an immediately physically dangerous situation, your instincts will lead directly to action, which is a survival mechanism. However, intuitions about a new path of inquiry, a solution, or a lifestyle change keep coming back until you make some kind of decision. These messages usually point to a positive growth step or to an expansion of who you really are. They frequently ask you to move out of your comfort zone into the unknown.

Ego-based drives are more often motivated by a sense of urgency—a desire to wrest control, to manipulate someone else, to "get what you want, and get it now." Fear-based thoughts rooted in unrealistic beliefs drain you, making you

> **"The physician does not learn everything he must know and master at high colleges alone; from time to time he must consult old women, gypsies, magicians, wayfarers, and all manner of peasant folk and random people, and learn from them; for these have more knowledge about such things than all the high colleges."**
> —Paracelsus, in Moore[3]

feel afraid, inadequate, limited, or *smaller*. Fear can also be a form of intuition that signals something that needs to be explored more fully and with more insight about the possible consequences.

Intuitive promptings will take you into the unknown, but an accompanying tingle of mysterious excitement usually helps dissipate unfounded fears.

Is intuition ever wrong?

Intuition is a natural attunement to knowledge that is meant to further our well-being and growth. In the beginning, we never know for sure the result of making a choice. Many high-level decision makers admit they aren't able to justify their gut feelings logically, but instinct seems to have positive results more often than not. Most of us get an intuition about something and run it by our logical process. We attempt to see what other options we have and weigh their priorities, but we choose the uncommon choice, after all. So many times, it's the uncommon choice that holds the key.

In retrospect, you may think an intuition led to the "wrong" choice. However, look again. Was it truly intuition speaking, or was it a fear-based choice after all? Intuitive guidance is there to take you to a deeper, higher, or more evolved place, and outcomes sometimes have to be assessed from a spiritual or cosmic perspective rather than our narrow judgments of good and bad.

People who hear voices that direct their lives, without integrating these experiences with their rational functions, are not necessarily functioning intuitively. While many mystics fit this description, most people in this category would probably be considered mentally ill.

How can I use intuition right now to get in touch with my life purpose?

The desire that prompted you to ask this question is already sorting information to find your answers. Remember, your purpose is inborn. It's not "out there." You are carrying it within you, and your best chance of finding it is to listen with as much quietude as you can. Let's say you are reading this workbook in bed, feeling depressed that tomorrow you have to get up and commute to a dead-end job. You feel frustrated. You want to do something now. You want directions about how to change your life for the better now! The following section describes an exercise that will help you to do that.

INTUITION EXERCISE

Choose a place where you won't be disturbed for a while. Get comfortable, close your eyes, and relax. Take a few breaths and begin to soften any muscles that feel tense. Take a few more deep inhalations. Allow your mind to slow down, little by little. Take your time. When you feel that you have entered a deeper, quieter space, write down a question in the space below:

✔ *I want to know . . .* _____

_____

_____

✔ *Describe how you feel about your life and your future.* _____

_____

_____

_____

✔ *Close your eyes and feel your body.* What sensations do you feel in your body? If your body could talk, what would it say right now?

_____

_____

_____

_____

✔ *If you are upset, write down what you are upset about.* Dump it out here. If you are outside in a place where you can lie down with your belly on the ground, this would be an excellent time to dump your "heavy" thoughts and energy into the Earth (who loves to receive energy from us, by the way!).

I am upset about . . . _____

_____

_____

_____

✔ *Become peaceful.* Close your eyes again and take a few deep breaths. Breathe in calming, refreshing air and send it down to your toes, and then bring it back up through your heart and let it go out again through the top of your skull. Still your thinking by mentally repeating "energy in, energy out" in synch with your breath. Let yourself fall into a lull.

✔ *What do I need now to be happy?* Close your eyes and let an answer come. Write down whatever your intuition tells you, no matter how odd it may seem. _____

_____

_____

_____

✔ *Ask again, What do I need now to be happy?* Close your eyes and ask your question again. Remain peaceful. Drift. Drift. Drift. Keep your attention on your breathing. What immediately comes to mind? Note fleeting impressions, images, messages, or single words. Anything. Let whatever arises emerge without judging it. Open your eyes and write down your thoughts. Repeat the process of asking for messages one or two more times. *After writing down your answers, forget about this exercise. You need not exert effort or struggle to hold on to what you received.*

_____

_____

_____

✔ *Trust that your process is working perfectly.* You may not understand the information you received in this exercise. It doesn't matter, for the answer will be made clear to you at some point. Your desire to know, by itself, raises your vibration to the level where you can attract what you need. This process allows you to get control of your negative emotions;

PAYING ATTENTION— MAKING A DIFFERENCE

"Rudolph J. (Rudy) Melone, a college president whose chance reading of a Chronicle article in 1978 about a small garlic-growing town in France inspired him to create the Gilroy Garlic Festival—transforming a sleepy California town into a world-famous city—has died . . . Dr. Melone was living in nearby Morgan Hill when he read . . . about Arleux, a small town in France which held an annual garlic festival and proclaimed itself Garlic Capital of the World. Knowing that garlic production in Gilroy . . . far surpassed any other region in the world, he conceived the idea of celebrating the 'stinking rose' at a bigger and better festival in Gilroy. The first festival in 1979 attracted about 25,000 people. 'No one at the time except Rudy thought to call it "The First Annual Festival," his wife, Gloria, recalled. 'But he was sure it was just the beginning.' Now more than 125,000 people from all over the world attend the three-day event each July, and the U.S. Department of Urban Affairs has proclaimed it a

release them; and create a quiet, still picture frame within which useful information may come forward. You're doing great!

✔ *Record your insights.* Write your thoughts on page 235 of the profile sheet.

_____

_____

INTUITION IS ALWAYS THERE

Intuition speaks to us in a quiet, persistent voice. To make use of this all-important guidance, get in the habit of doing the following three-part exercise each day, or at least once a week:

1. *Send the universe your request for information on any matter. Ask for help on a specific question or ask to accomplish something easily.*
2. *Notice whom you meet. Listen for any relevant information or answers.*
3. *Take an action in the direction of the information you receive.*

The Three-Part Intuition Process Key Exercise

1. *Listen for the still, small voice:*
   • Before leaping out of bed in the morning, stay quiet and close your eyes.
   • Breathe energy in, breathe problems out.
2. *To accomplish your top priorities for the day:*
   • Ask yourself, "What do I most want to accomplish today?"

• Notice your immediate inner thought about what is a top priority. You may be surprised. For example, if you have been thinking you want to find your life purpose (an ongoing priority) and your next thought is "take the cat to the hospital and let the children on the cancer ward play with him" (something you had been toying with doing), follow your intuition to find out about hospitals that are open to this kind of "pet therapy." Who knows, you might meet someone there who opens you to a new way of thinking, or you may be so moved by the children that your life is transformed. Often, when we are moved to give, we receive far more in the bargain than we feel we are giving.

> model festival. The core of the event is the generosity of more than 5,000 volunteers who work hundreds of jobs earning an hourly wage, which they then donate to charities of their choice. As a result, the event has raised more than $5 million for local philanthropies."
> *San Francisco Chronicle*[4]

• Either complete your top priority action in the morning or as soon as possible, or take one step toward it before "life errands" deplete your energy. Completing something gives you an energy boost. Procrastination is draining. On the other hand, if you act when you are tired or depressed, results are usually not very satisfactory either.

3. *Determine what you most need help with and ask for it!*
   • Examples: "Today I need courage, memory, and mental brilliance to pass my exams effortlessly." "God, please stay close today."
   • Trust that your needs are being met in the best and fastest way possible for your highest good. Let the universe handle the details.

SUBJECTS OF INTEREST TO ME

Jot down each day for thirty days:
✔ Anything that you overhear, read, think about, see, or are told about *that catches your attention more than usual.*
✔ Things that excite, delight, encourage, intrigue, or uplift you.
✔ A brief description of someone whom you admire. Why do you admire him or her?

✔ Any need you see in your environment that is not being addressed.

Date

1. _____

2. _____

3. _____

4. _____

5. _____

6. _____

7. _____

8. _____

9. _____

10. _____

11. _____

12. _____

13. _____

14. _____

15. _____

16. _____

17. _____

18. _____

19. _____

20. _____

21. _____

22. _____

23. _____

24. _____

25. _____

26. _____

27. _____

28. _____

29. _____

30. _____

✔ Summarize any pattern you see in your notes. Underline the sentence or words that give you a feeling of excitement or arouse strong interest. Write down these insights on page 235 of the profile sheet.

LOUELLA'S STORY

"I had been depressed for four months. I'd been unemployed again for the fifth time. I am an English major from U.C. Berkeley, and I'd had administrative jobs in the environmental field, working for a property management firm and an asbestos removal contractor. I did well, but I knew it wasn't my life's work. I'd get a job, and then would be bored, get the next job and be bored all over again. I didn't want to repeat that cycle.

> " 'I have forgotten something,' said a man to the Sufi poet Rumi. 'There is one thing that must never be forgotten,' Rumi replied. 'It is as if a king had sent you to a foreign country with a task to perform. You go and perform many other tasks. But if you fail to perform the task for which you were sent, it will be as if you had done nothing at all.' "
>
> — Harry R. Moody[5]

"A friend called me who was reading *The Purpose of Your Life* and said, 'This is your life, Louella!' I was at the point of drifting aimlessly, thinking I was keeping all my options open. But after reading about intention in the book, I thought, I need to set the direction of what I want. I wanted to be shown what to do, but I had no memory of a passion.

I did the exercise about what I loved to do the most, which was to play the piano. Recognizing that passion for the piano helped me form an intention to put out to the universe. I also started doing the exercise '*Today I want to meet good people.*' I started playing the piano more, and even began to watch *Oprah* and her Change-Your-Life TV.

"One day I went to the shopping mall to get a couple of books I had seen on her show for my mother, and as I went in, I saw a new music store. Suddenly, I felt like it was calling my name. I went in and asked to have the newest digital piano demonstrated to me. When the supervisor joined us, I asked him a complicated question that he couldn't answer. But I figured it out myself on the computer screen. He said jokingly, 'You should work here.' It didn't hit me immediately, and then when it registered, I touched his arm and said, 'Are you hiring?' and he said, 'Of course.'

"I met the manager the next day. I explained that I had no sales experience and confessed that I wasn't that great of a piano player, but she said, 'Never mind. You have a great personality. I want you to start tomorrow." She also said — which made me tingle — 'You remind me of myself when I started working here.' Before she was hired there, she had been on disability and depressed over a family death. She had heard the salesman playing the piano outside the store, and commented, 'What a great job you have. I would do that even if I didn't get paid,' and he said, 'Would you like to work here?' "

Insights from Louella's Story

- She recognized her old pattern of taking any job without much intention, which led to boredom.
- She allowed herself to feel depressed and aimless, without rushing out to find another job.

- She received a synchronistic phone call from a friend, who suggested she read *The Purpose of Your Life* because it discussed people's stories that were similar to her story.
- She took action, bought the book, examined her life, and "remembered" her passion for the piano.
- She made a clear intention to connect with her passion without knowing how that would happen but trusting that something would show up.
- Following her intuition to buy books for her mother, she passed a new store that seemed to call out to her.
- Following her interest in new digital pianos (*part of her passion for music and the piano*), she stepped into her new job *effortlessly*.
- She loves her work.

✔ What stood out for you in Louella's story? Jot down your insight on page 236 of the profile sheet.

PERCEIVING AND LIVING THE "RULES OF THE ROAD"

Review the Rules of the Road on page 136 (excerpted from *The Purpose of Your Life*, page 31). *Use the exercise following the box to apply them to your current situation.*

Apply the Rules of the Road for Effortless Success

Write the Rules of the Road on separate index cards, and take them with you during the day. You might wish to select one "rule" a day for the next twelve days and notice anything that relates to or confirms the idea you are working on that day. Write down your observations on the back of that card, date it, and keep the cards together. The perceptions you record on the daily index cards will begin to instill these principles into your thinking at a deep level. Over time, you won't even think about them anymore, but they will be operating more effectively for you than were your former, limiting beliefs. You'll gain self-confidence, a more positive and patient attitude, and a brighter self-image, which will attract more and more abundance, vitality, and opportunity. Even though you will be investing time into this process, the results may feel almost effortless.

RULES OF THE ROAD
FOR LIVING YOUR LIFE PURPOSE

Keep these ideas in mind when you are feeling confused or need a little support in taking new steps. To evaluate your current thinking, check each box for which you can say "yes" to the accompanying statement. If you don't agree, you might want to write out how you feel or what your experience has been.

❑   I believe that my attitudes and beliefs structure how my world appears to me.

❑   I am absolutely clear that I want to live in the flow of my purpose.

❑   I can honestly admit what is working in my life and what is not.

❑   I believe that my intuition is guiding me to fulfill my purpose.

❑   I will commit to taking small steps toward the things that have heart and meaning for me.

❑   I can let go of struggling for power and trying to control others.

❑   I remember to keep things simple.

❑   I believe that everyone has at least one natural talent that is necessary to the working of the universal flow.

❑   I believe that my world can change as I change my attitudes and beliefs, and that anything is possible.

❑   I attract people and events at the appropriate time.

❑   I always have a choice.

If you can honestly check off every box, your purpose has already emerged or is very close to being revealed to you. If there are any statements you cannot check, begin to hold these ideas in your mind, and make an intention to have these insights clarified through direct experience. When in doubt or under stress, review these Rules of the Road.

WHEN YOU ARE FEELING SUCCESSFUL
AND ENERGIZED

Be sure to track your successes to foster self-confidence and trust. Answer some or all of the questions in this section when you're "on a roll and feeling terrific!"

1. The best contribution I made today was . . . Why? _____

   _____

2. I was in the flow of my life purpose today when . . . _____

   _____

3. What is working great in my life is . . . _____

   _____

   What is not working very well for me is . . . _____

   _____

4. The intuitive message, (or hunch) that I received today was . . .

   _____

   _____

5. My ability to be present increased today because . . . _____

   _____

6. I let go of trying to control . . . _____

   _____

7. I simplified my life by . . . _____

   _____

8. My natural talent for _____ helped me flow with life today.

   _____

9. I believe that anything is possible about situation X. The best result I can think of is . . . _____

   _____

   _____

10. I attracted exactly what I needed today. (What was it?) _____

_____

_____

11. The most beneficial choice I made today was . . . _____

_____

_____

12. What interested me most today was . . . _____

_____

_____

Record your answers to 1, 2, and 3 on page 236 of the profile sheet.

THE INNER MASCULINE AND INNER FEMININE

Inside each of us—both men and women—is the capacity to be assertive, dynamic, logical, analytical, and productive (often referred to metaphorically as masculine energy. On the other hand, we also have the ability to be receptive, magnetic, intuitive, expressive, and visionary (the complementary feminine energy). The terms *masculine* and *feminine* are symbolic representations of energy states and do not refer to external physical genders. Our ability to act creatively depends on how these two qualities interact within us. When balanced, the two energy states working together—dynamic assertive energy and magnetic receptive energy—create successful action and satisfaction. If either side becomes too dominant, it throws us off and creates a feeling of being overwhelmed, as well as a state of frustration, helplessness, hopelessness, or meaninglessness.

One way to become aware of how our inner masculine and feminine qualities are working is to look at our external life and try to determine which side is more in evidence.

External Conditions Are a Mirror of Our Internal Condition

Masculine is dominant.
Are you driven to accomplish, control time, or make plans? Do you tend to be critical of yourself and others? Do you have an impressive to-do list? These are strong signs that your masculine is driving you. If you are feeling frustrated, overwhelmed, and out of control, it's likely that you are giving yourself too many demands and don't have the

inner resources right now to meet them directly. Your masculine is not able to meet the demands you have placed on "him." You need to back off, slow down, ask for help, delegate, reassess your goals, and get back in touch with your priorities.

For example, Brenda, a software programmer, was feeling drained, overwhelmed, and angry at having two of her projects fall through. She had begun to work with her masculine and feminine sides in therapy. On reflection, Brenda realized it was her masculine side that was worn down and feeling ineffective. Her masculine side, which is responsible for meeting deadlines and coming up with solutions based on analytical processes, had gotten her quick promotions in the past. But now "he" was working even harder and enjoying it less. This highly competitive and controlling attitude was no longer serving Brenda's needs. One could say that Brenda was driven by her "out-of-control" masculine side because she was out of touch with her feminine side.

Feminine is dominant.

On the other hand, do you often ask yourself what is the point of doing certain things? Do you crave more beauty? More balance? Have you slowed down? Are you depressed? Do you spend a lot of time day-dreaming, writing in your journal, or expressing your creativity? Are you deeply interested in probing relationship issues or reading or writing poetry, or are you feeling restless for a deeper kind of life? If so, you are being heavily influenced by your magnetic, receptive feminine side. For example, Grant was deeply involved in his spiritual practice and unwilling to take any job that didn't feel "transformative" (his words). He longed for a soulmate, and he spent hours in deep conversations with friends and writing in his journal about life and the meaning of it all. He felt he was too evolved for most mundane work, and he spent hours working on paintings that he claimed were too special for the general art market. Grant was caught up in an unconscious fascination with his feminine side.

What to do?

The first step in creating balance, of course, is to become aware of the imbalance. Remember, it is our internal condition that creates the external scenario of our lives. Our external world looks the way it does because of the way we perceive it through the lenses of our beliefs, attitudes, and past experiences.

Brenda decided to look within and seek her answers from what she found there. She decided to have a talk with her masculine and feminine inner voices by doing the meditation below. After her internal dialogue with these inner figures, Brenda arrived at the conclusion that even though she was doing well at her job, she had begun to resent the policies of the company and therefore didn't feel connected to what she was doing (she was out of touch with what mattered to her, which is always given to us by our feminine nature). Therefore, Brenda asked her inner feminine side what she wanted most at this point in life, and she received this guidance: "What about the light?" Brenda considered this answer for a few days, and after an important dream, she realized that the message referred to her earlier aspirations to work with blind children (Brenda had a blind sibling). Life for Brenda had become unrewarding and dry. Therefore, she had to give her masculine creative energy something more worthwhile to do, which is determined by the feminine voice of the soul. Brenda took a part-time job and began training herself in her new field.

Grant, also in a therapeutic setting, began to get in touch with his needs to come down to earth a little and to gain stability by taking a job in the graphics department of a medical publishing company. He still painted and wrote in his journal, but the simple discipline of showing up for work every day and performing tasks successfully began to reinforce a more satisfying connection with himself and the everyday world, which fueled greater productivity in his creative life.

The Voice of Soul (Feminine Energy) and Spirit (Masculine Energy)

Read the following steps and then close your eyes, relax, and allow images to come into your mind's eye. Soft music in the background may help you to concentrate.

1. Take a few deep breaths. Let all thoughts gently drift away. Allow your mind to become still.

2. Go into the center of your being. Continue to breathe gently, and empty the mind.

3. Imagine an empty stage with a chair sitting in the middle of the space. Invite in your feminine quality: let her appear in any image that arises. You may see a person or hear a voice or see a symbol. Do not judge what you receive, but be eager to accept whatever your imagina-

tion wants to provide. Every detail of the images, sounds, or messages you receive has significance. Notice the state of your inner feminine quality. Hold the image and ask her these questions:

- How does she *feel?*
- What does she need?
- What is her highest priority?
- What is her vision for your life?
- Ask any further questions about the purpose of your life at this point—then thank her for coming.

4. Now bring another chair onto the stage, next to your feminine symbol, and invite your masculine quality. Again, allow any person, symbol, sound, or message to appear without judgment. Hold the image and ask him these questions:

- How *successful* is he? (Be sure to give him your full attention and respect.)
- Is he willing and able to carry out the vision of your soul's feminine voice?
- Why or why not? What does he need? (Get him to give you a specific statement about what he needs to carry out your feminine's plans.)
- What would make him a stronger, more effective force in your life?

When you feel complete, thank both of them for visiting you, and bring your awareness back to the present.

5. Write down your insights. _____

_____

_____

_____

_____

✔ Summarize your insights about the values your feminine thinks are important and the kind of help your masculine energy has requested on page 236 of the profile sheet.

CLEAR CONFUSION: BECOME A MAGNET
FOR WHAT YOU WANT

- Create a moratorium on worry. Dedicate the next week to having a good time every day.
- Step back mentally from all your troubles just for today.
- Pick one person in your life, and mentally send him or her loving appreciation once a day.
- Get more sleep.
- Do one fun thing for yourself every single day.

MAKE THE MOST OF SYNCHRONICITY

- Do one new thing this week.
- Notice who comes to mind today. No doubt that person is thinking of you. Check in with someone who cares about you. If you can't think of one person who cares about you, your top priority is to have some fun this week! Get out to a new café and introduce yourself to one new person. Go to a bookstore lecture and meet the author. Get a massage. Invite someone to tea. Loosen up!
- Put yourself "on assignment" to receive exactly the information you need today.
- Don't forget to repeat "Today I want to meet good people!" every morning. Every evening send loving energy to everyone who met you during the day, everyone who is thinking about you, and everyone who is important in your life.
- Trust that nothing happens by accident. If you have something you're working on, or need a solution, notice who calls you. Probe the connection a little bit. If it seems appropriate, ask any callers if they know something about this issue.
- If you don't understand why a certain coincidence occurred, ask yourself, "If this were a dream, how would I interpret it?" What was the beginning, middle, and end of this story? What title would I give this event? What did this happening prompt me to do, to think about, to learn?

Make a TIP CARD of anything you have read in this section that excited or inspired you.

THE PERSONAL YEAR CYCLE

The numerological Personal Year is an indicator of what to do for success and how to work with any challenges we encounter. Based on the ancient Pythagorean system of numerical symbolism, this system allows us to find where we are currently and even look ahead to opportunities in the coming year. The cycles are nine years long, after which the sequence is repeated.

To find your Personal Year, simply add your month and day of birth to the current year:

For example, if Donna, born November 29, 1945, wants to know what her personal year is for 1998, she adds

November 29 to 1998: 11 (Nov.) + 29 + 1998 = (1+1+2+9+1+9+9+8) = 40 (4+0=4)

Donna is in a Four Personal Year in 1998.

The numbers follow in sequence and begin in January of each year.

PERSONAL YEAR INDICATIONS, ACTIVITIES, LESSONS

1 Planning, launching, moving, beginning, new opportunities, independence. Favors mental activities, writing, starting a new business. Challenges: arrogance, courage, confusion, self-confidence. Action months: April, September.

2 Relationships, cooperation, details, slow change, receptivity. Favors love, integration, negotiating. Challenges: fear, patience, sluggishness, overlooking details, oversubmissiveness. Action months: March, August, December.

3 Good luck, creativity, teamwork, social contacts, self-improvement, happiness, travel. Good for sales. Challenges: overoptimism, distractions, jealousy, extravagance. Action months: February, July, November.

4 Planning, building, revitalizing health and image, taking care of business. Favors reorganizing, buying investments, repairing.

Challenges: health concerns, debts, stress, restrictions. Action months: January, June, October.

5 Sudden changes, new opportunities, freedom, love affairs, public activity. Favors selling, promotion, multiple projects, vitality, sex. Challenges: distractions, lending money, exhaustion. Action months: May, August, September.

6 Responsibility, marriage or divorce, duties. Favors teaching, improving the home, paying back loans, teamwork. Challenges: feeling like a victim, resentment, guilt, deadlines, money. Action months: April, August.

7 Reflection, self-growth, education, desire for nature. Favors research, writing, increasing spiritual-intuitive growth, meditation. Challenges: self-deception, pessimism, loss, deceit. Action months: March, July, December.

8 Recognition, career fulfillment, investments, licensure, increased income. Favors editing, buying and selling property. Challenges: money, legal matters, power struggles, overextension. Action months: February, June, November.

9 Completion, change for the better, opportunities, expansion. Favors healing, education, long-distance travel, spirituality. Challenges: emotions, loss, compassion, tolerance, letting go. Action months: January, May, September.

Notes about your Personal Year: How might your life purpose be taking shape according to your Personal Year? If you wish, make notes also on page 236 of the profile sheet.

Books and Tapes That People Recommend to Me

List here the books that people tell you about. I always pay attention when someone tells me about an interesting book, and when two or more people tell me about the same book, I race out to the bookstore immediately! _____

_____

_____

_____

_____

_____

CHAPTER 10

Fun Stuff—Make Your Own Oracles

⌒∞⌒

"I discovered that five basic shapes appear in the art of all cultures: the circle, the square, the triangle, the cross, and the spiral. . . . different cultures do give similar meanings to these shapes. The circle symbolizes wholeness, the square indicates stability, the triangle represents goals and dreams, the cross stands for relationship, and the spiral means growth. It also became evident to me that the meaning attributed to each shape stands for a process of human growth, and the shape carries this process within itself."

ANGELES ARRIEN[1]

If you would like to have a fun way of developing your intuitive understanding of symbolic messages, you can make any of the three sets of oracle cards described in this chapter. Especially when you are going through an uncertain time, it's helpful to create a special quiet time when you can mentally ask a question, such as "What do I need to become aware of now?" Pull one, three, or seven cards to find the synchronistic message for the day.

Tarot cards are probably the best-known oracle cards. No one knows where tarot originated. Tarot is divided into 22 Major Arcana (Higher Wisdom) cards, which, when drawn by the seeker, speak to important issues of change, growth, and spiritual development. The other fifty cards cover a range of mundane events, influences, and portents through the four suits: Swords (mental plane), Cups (emotional plane), Wands (spiritual plane), and Pentacles or Disks (physical plane).

The cards you draw, whether they be tarot cards or ones you make yourself, usually speak to current influences in your life rather than forecasting future events; however, you may also find that they sometimes have an uncanny tendency to mirror your unfolding future.

You may wish to purchase tarot cards, runes (Nordic stone oracles), a book on the *I Ching* (an ancient Chinese oracle), angel cards, or any other divination tools that help you practice intuitive interpretation. Remember, your own inner interpretation is your best source of wisdom, although there are many good books on oracles. One of the best is Angeles Arrien's *Tarot Handbook*,[2] used with the Thoth tarot deck.

ORACLE NO. 1: GUIDING PRINCIPLES

Write the following guiding principles on separate index cards and keep them handy. When you want guidance, mix up your stack and pick one or two cards without looking at them. How does the guiding principle selected apply to the present moment?

There is a purpose already within you.
There is a purposefulness to whatever you are going through.
Doing what you love to do puts you in the flow of synchronicity.
What you focus on expands.
What you have is what you want.
Be at peace with what is.
You are already complete.
Universal Intelligence is perfect and operates with effortless ease.
You always have a choice.
Set your intention and ask for support.
Let the universe handle the details.
Trust the process.
I will take responsibility for the things and people in my life without blaming others.
I will practice acceptance of everything that occurs.
I will practice giving something to everyone I meet.
I will practice gratitude for the things and people in my life.
I will keep my thoughts, language, and actions focused on what I wish to attract.
I will look for guidance in intuitions, synchronicities, and dreams.
I will let go of trying to control people and events.
I will look for the lesson in everything that happens.
My life is part of the larger world plan.

ORACLE NO. 2: SYNCHRONICITY WORDS

Following is a list of 28 sets of contrary ideas. If you have a computer, you can use your label format to write individual labels for *each word*. Next, stick one word from a pair onto **the top of a 3 × 5 index card. Turn the card upside down and stick the opposite word from the pair on the opposite side (see illustration).** If you aren't able to make labels, simply write one word of the pair on the top and bottom of each card. Feel free to add your own words or take out words.

Before committing to making these word cards, read about Oracle No. 3. If you want to use the word cards with images as suggested in Oracle No. 3, you will need to put your words onto 5 × 7 index cards.

How to Use the Synchronicity Cards

1. Ask a specific question, such as "what do I need to know about the possibility of going back to school?" Try to avoid asking questions that require a yes or no answer, such as "Should I go back to school?" That puts too much pressure on you to interpret the cards you draw. What you want from your synchronicity cards is helpful information that *expands your thinking* about the question, rather than a prophetic answer.

2. After forming your question, it's a good idea to write it down in your journal.

3. Shuffle the pack of cards, and without looking draw one card.

4. What does the card seem to mean in relation to your question?

5. Write the word from the card you drew as the answer to your question, and then let your mind free-associate from that word. Continue writing without controlling your ideas. What emerges?

6. You can continue to draw cards for a total of three to seven words. Does a sentence or thought emerge? Have fun!

ORACLE NO. 3: SYNCHRONICITY WORDS AND IMAGES

To make an even more interesting oracle, add images to your word cards. **Put the words on 5 × 7 index cards**, which will leave a big blank space in the middle of the card. Next, begin collecting postcards with provocative images until you have a large stack of twenty to eighty

```
+-----------+        +-----------+
|   Stop    |        |   Power   |
|           |        |           |
|           |        |           |
|    oÐ     |        |   plǝᴉʎ    |
+-----------+        +-----------+
```

stop/go	power/yield	beginning/ending	illusion/birth
change/direct	yes/no	letting go/hanging on	conserve/spend
escape/stay	yes/yes	seclusion/isolation	projection/authenticity
love/fear	signal/meaning	holding on/release	outward/inward
crossing/parting	home/strange	entering/leaving	becoming/undoing
wait/move	praise/truth	success/failure	alignment/confusion
lead/retreat	respond/deny	poised/action	discrimination/judgment
alone/support	receive/give	hope/hesitate	victim/aggressor
threshold/barrier	habit/release	dream/imagine	opportunity/illusion
up/down	broaden/narrow	control/surrender	integrity/ungrounded
laughter/guilt	forgive/resent	eliminate/foster	examine/understand
anger/belittle	explore/limit	growth/limitation	distraction/goal
difficulty/ease	hide/show	compulsion/freedom	apologize/aggravate
anxious/fearless	know/believe	new/old	information/intuition
expand/contract	first/last	conform/rebel	wonderful/lacking
share/hoard	desire/intention	stand/fall	promise/miracle
sexual/abstinent	self/others	conflict/peace	communication/move
open/closed	man/woman	willing/resistant	obstacle/solution
phase/time	folly/wisdom	shame/value	organize/disperse
east/west	distortion/clarity	conviction/doubt	engage/withdraw
energy/skill	victory/loss	wealth/necessity	blind spot/memory
journey/chase	up/down	moderation/boldness	expectations/dread
begin/complete	day/night	progress/stagnation	perseverance/effort
faith/discovery	force/relinquish	month/week	achievement/decision
trust/question	soon/later	mother/father	child/adult
son/daughter	in/out	north/south	yes/yes
success/success	no/no	go/stay	blame/praise
men/women	yes/no	yes/no	stay/go

postcards. You can also make your own "postcards" by pasting images cut out of magazines onto 5 × 7 cards that have been trimmed down to 4 × 6 inches. These image cards should fit into the space between the word pairs on the 5 × 7 cards you have already made.

How to Use The Word and Image Cards Together

1. Again, ask a specific question, such as "What do I need to know about the possibility of going back to school?"

2. If you like, write the question in your journal to keep a record of your process.

3. Separately shuffle each deck of word cards and image cards.

4. Concentrating on your question, pull one card from each deck without looking at them.

5. Turn over each card. Put the image card in the middle of your two words.

6. The upright word at the top of your card is the operative word. It's okay to turn the image card right side up if it's upside down.

7. Free-associate to the combination of the word and the image. What does your intuition suggest? One method is to write down your response and continue writing free-association style. Otherwise, continue to draw two more sets of word cards with images on top, for a total of three sets. If you draw more than three sets, you may dilute the message and feel confused. If you don't get a message after three sets, you aren't ready to hear this answer yet! Record insights for one month on pages 236–237 of the profile sheet.

INTUITIVE READING OF ANOTHER
PERSON'S QUESTION

Another intriguing method of gleaning answers from your inner wisdom is to work with a partner who also wants guidance. You can do this in your study group or with a good friend whom you trust and who generally has a positive attitude.

Step 1: Each person writes his or her question on the top of a blank piece of paper.

Step 2: Exchange papers and read each other's question, making sure you understand the other person's question and he or she understands yours.

Step 3: At the same time, each person begins to write an answer to the other person's question. Resist the temptation to speak, joke, or laugh! Keep your pen moving and let your thoughts flow freely. Don't stop to wonder if the writing makes sense. Keep writing until you run out of things to say. You'll know when to stop.

Step 4: Read your intuitive answer to the other person. It may make sense to him or her, but not to you! Let the other person read his or her message about your question.

PART FOUR

FEARS
AND OBSTACLES

CHAPTER 11

Downloading and Offloading Fears, Blocks, and Resistances

For years, early morning was a time I dreaded. In the process of waking up, my mind would run with panic. All the worries of the previous day would still be with me, spinning around with old regrets as well as fears for the future. I don't know how or when the change came, but now when I emerge from night, it is with more hope than fear. I try to get outside as early as possible so that I can look for signs of first light, the faint, muddy red of dawn.

—KATHLEEN NORRIS[1]

It is human nature to look for the reasons that things happen. Particularly when we want to move forward to more fulfillment and recognition, better health and relationships, and financial abundance—*and it's not happening*—we naturally assume we must have some inner blocks. We think, "Maybe I have a fear of success," or "maybe I have a fear of failure," or "maybe I sabotage myself because I don't feel I deserve to succeed." Over the years of listening to people talk about their blocks, I've started to wonder just how real these blocks are. Perhaps we give them too much attention and energy. Perhaps we could try to relax a little and shift our focus to seeing ourselves as whole and worthwhile—blocks and all. Maybe we could give up *feeding* the belief in blocks and the old fantasy of having to "fix ourselves" in order to be perfect. Rather, we could give more attention to trying new behavior. Personal development coach Max Wellspring put it like this: "I've learned not to give so much energy to perceived blocks. Instead, I take another tack. Now, I turn it over to the wisdom of the higher self, or whatever you want to call it. Instead of trying to figure it out and fix it, I look for guidance. As I develop trust, it's a self-perpetuating system. That feeling of low-level anxiety starts to recede and quiet down as I listen for the answers to come. Sometimes, I hear something that I would call an internal directive. Other times, it's more like a feeling of know-ingness about what to try next. I've had so many synchronicities come into play, I know this works. It's not just a theory anymore. I've lived it. I really try to practice this method from heartbeat to heartbeat. I can't imagine doing it any other way now.

"When I left my so-called secure job with the law firm, I went through an incredible amount of anxiety about how my future would unfold. At first, I had to do it more consciously, but now it's more sec-ond nature. Now when I have life questions, I try to set aside time to light a candle, sit with my journal, and wait for the ideas to come through the writing."

Of course, there are certain unresolved life issues that can be healed only with professional psychotherapy. Aside from these instances, our so-called blocks sometimes dissolve simply from paying more attention to thinking, speaking, and acting in a more positive way.

Another reason things may not work out the way we wish is that our timing is a bit off: We are ahead of ourselves, or conversely we've let an opportunity slip by. It's helpful to remember that even when we are dis-couraged and feel helpless to know which way to turn, our purpose is *still* quietly preparing the next door for us to walk through. Everything has a purpose, and anything is possible.

In *The Purpose of Your Life*, therapist Colleen McGovern shares the story of the healing of her niece, E., who was violently raped while attending a U.S. federal academy. Even though this was a highly charged issue requiring professional treatment, E.'s story provides a number of insights about the healing power of working on beliefs. Fol-lowing is a summary of what E. eventually learned:

- *That she had real options.* In the past, she had always painted a pic-ture of herself as having few options or resources because she had had an alcoholic father and a very old-fashioned mother.
- *That she could change her belief.* Before her therapy, she believed that the only way to get an education was to continue at the acad-emy, in spite of suffering such a traumatic experience there.
- *That her desire to feel safe and happy was normal and that she deserved to get an education and feel safe.* She had had few role models of successful people in her life. No other family members had gone to college; feeling "less than," she thought she had to

"put up" with the federal academy because she was on scholar-ship.

- *To identify how she wanted to feel without having to come up with a solution about how to achieve that feeling.*
- *To keep her focus on how she wanted to feel.* E. practiced visualizing going to a school somewhere that felt as good as when she visited her aunt in California. She didn't try to figure out where that school was.
- *That she could attract the support she needed without struggling.* Eventually, E. received some tuition money from family members, was accepted at another school, and found part-time student employment and a homey place to live.
- *That even this severe trauma served a purpose.* Eventually, it empowered her to help others and find a deeper meaning in life. After making the transition to the new school, E. went on to establish a rape crisis center in Newport, Rhode Island.
- *That there is a greater plan at work in our lives.* E. came to realize that the academy had never been right for her. In the long run, the painful event had precipitated a change for the better and enabled her to help others.

WORKING THROUGH FEAR OR FRUSTRATION

If, like E., you are feeling stuck, frustrated, helpless, or depressed about something you perceive to be negative and unchangeable, use the following questions to help shift your awareness. You can answer all of them in sequence, or choose one or two questions; write for five minutes to see what comes up. You can also turn the questions into a simple meditation for use in study group meetings. If you use the questions in a guided visualization, simply add meditative music and have someone lead the group in closing their eyes, relaxing, and opening to their intuitive guidance. After the meditation, each person can write down the information received.

✔ *Tell the truth.* What would you like to have happen in your life?

_____

_____

_____

✔ *Pay attention.* What do you know about this situation? What has to change? _____

_____

_____

_____

✔ *Feel the fear.* What is your worst fear at this moment? For example, "I'm afraid that I will never find my life purpose. I'm afraid that I will be stuck doing something below my abilities forever. I'm afraid that I don't have what it takes to succeed." _____

_____

_____

✔ *Locate the source of the fear.* Where do you think the fear comes from? _____

_____

_____

✔ *Name the voice of the fear.* Does the voice of the fear seem to origi- nate from your inner tyrant? Inner critic? Inner child? Your mother? Your father? _____

_____

✔ *Rewrite the fear into a positive statement.* For example, if the fear is *I'm afraid that I will be stuck doing something below my abilities for- ever,* rewrite it in your own words to say something like this: *Life is presenting me with wonderful opportunities to get paid for what I love to do—and what I do well.*

TAKE THE HIT AS A GIFT

George Leonard and Michael Murphy have a wonderful exercise in *The Life We Are Given: A Long-Term Program for Realizing the Poten- tial of Body, Mind, Heart, and Soul* called Taking the Hit As a Gift. They write: "Unexpected blows come in many varieties, from the merely bothersome to the profound. . . . Our most common responses to such unfortunate happenings tend to make things worse."[2] They note that we usually have an immediate counterattack and fight back reflexively. Or we may whine, play the victim role, or simply deny that we felt anything, getting into the habit of turning off or minimizing our feelings.

Instead, Leonard recommends the kind of response often used in martial arts: to fully experience and acknowledge the strong feelings, *and use the energy of these feelings to handle the situation at hand*. In the exercise, two partners work together. One person stands with feet shoulder-width apart, balanced and centered, with arm out to a forty-five-degree angle. The other person walks up quietly behind him, and without warning simultaneously grabs the arm and makes a loud shout, continuing to hold the wrist firmly (without pulling the person off balance).

Leonard says: "Be totally aware of how the sudden hit affected you. Speaking aloud in a clear voice, describe exactly what is going on within you. Specify exactly where in your body each feeling or sensation is located. Don't look at your partner as you speak. Resist the temptation to point the finger of your free hand at different parts of your body. Use words only, and be as specific as possible. For example: 'When you grabbed me, I jumped and blinked both eyes. My heart seemed to jump up into my throat. Now my throat feels a little dry. I can feel the pressure of your hands on my right wrist. . . . My abdomen feels tight. My breathing is shallower than usual.' " As you keep speaking, you'll notice that the conditions you've been describing melt away. "Many people discover that merely becoming aware of an imbalance tends to correct it," Leonard concludes.[4]

> **"As the planet farthest out in the solar system, Pluto symbolizes the deepest, most profound level of change possible in the human psyche. It is the primordial feminine power that intrudes on consciousness and cannot be placated by will or reason. . . . She symbolizes the deep inward journey that each of us embarks upon after losing something precious. For most of us, this is not done consciously or willingly, but by inner forces that compel us to enter the purifying fire that separates one level of existence from another."**
> —Barbara Schermer[3]

The Hit Adds Energy

The second part of the exercise encourages you to notice that the sudden hit has *added energy* to your body and your psyche. "As a result of being startled," writes Leonard, "your entire nervous system has come to the alert. You've been shaken out of whatever lethargy might have previously held you in check. Now you can choose what positive uses you wish to make of the extra energy that is yours to use.

"Take a series of deep breaths," he advises. "Move up and down rhythmically by bending and unbending your knees. Become aware of

> " 'I [Chan Khong] have a lot of energy. It is the energy of the Tiger. We must know how to make use of, to transform, that energy. . . . it can be very destructive. . . . It has taken me a lot of time to transform it. . . . With mindful living we slow down our acts so we can observe our habit energies, we transform the negative ones and cultivate the positive ones in order to live in harmony with others.'
>
> "Chan Khong . . . was taught to defer to her older sisters, but she could not . . . from the time she was a little girl, Sister Chan Khong had a mind of her own. At age fourteen she began working with poor children in the slums of Saigon. She did not meet Thich Nhat Hanh, her teacher, until she was twenty-one. She had no dream of being known by others, she was simply a very devout Buddhist teenager, and she knew that she wanted to help children who were going hungry and becoming delinquents. This is where her Tiger energy was helpful, she said. No one could stop her, though they tried."
>
> —China Galland[6]

the extra energy you now possess. Even the tight grip on your wrist is giving you energy. Begin moving around with a feeling of power. Your partner may be having trouble holding you. In any case, ask your partner to release your wrist and walk around the room expansively, arms open. Ask yourself if you have more energy now than when you started the exercise."[5]

A mild example of translating a hit into useful activity is reported by a man named Malcolm, who remarked, "Last night I got a wrong number at 4:30 A.M., which always gives me a bit of a scare, thinking it's my kids calling. Then I put the phone back off the cradle, and it started making that irritating beeping sound. By then, I knew I wasn't going back to sleep, so I went out and started surfing the Internet. I found a great hotel room on Maui for my next vacation!"

✔ Make a TIP CARD: Remember George Leonard's exercise the next time you "take a hit." Jot down a note to yourself on an index card: *I will remember to feel and describe to myself all the feelings when I take a "hit" or unexpected physical or emotional blow. I will notice where and how the hit has actually added energy.*

WHAT DID YOU GET CRITICIZED FOR?

Sometimes, the very things we were criticized for in childhood are a precursor of our later life purpose. For example, as a child, Chicago musician Steve Cooper was frequently scolded by his mother for spending too much time sitting on the floor of his room and fooling around with his record collection. "Watch out," she said. "You're never going to make a living doing that." How wrong she was! Today, Steve, a successful and well-known bandleader, has appeared on *Oprah* as well as played music for many top-notch television shows. How many successful authors or playwrights were told, "Go outside and play. You read too much!" How many artists or inventors were scolded by their mothers for dragging all kinds of funky things into their room?

✔ What did people say about you as a child? _____

_____

_____

_____

✔ What, if anything did you get criticized for? Has this so-called flaw turned out to be an asset or part of your life purpose? _____

_____

_____

_____

✔ Record whatever you'd like from this exercise on page 237 of the profile sheet.

NANCY'S STORY

Nancy P., a former public speaking coach for a large company, a wife, and a mother of three, hit a wall when her husband walked into the kitchen one night and announced that he no longer had a job. His company, a huge international chemical company, had laid off his small department. "I'll never forget that day. We had just finished our dream house and expected to live there the rest of our lives. My life as I knew it had ended, but I didn't know that at that moment."

Nancy explained that during this

> "Repentance is not a popular word these days, but I believe that many of us recognize it when it strikes us in the gut. Repentance is coming to our senses, seeing suddenly, what we've done that we might not have done, or recognizing, as Oscar Wilde says in his great religious meditation *De Profundis,* that the problem is not in what we do but in what we become."
> —Kathleen Norris[7]

time of readjustment, as her husband tried to find another job, she never once asked herself, "What do I want?" "He'd ask me at the dinner table, and I drew a blank. I just said, 'You're the one who is bringing in most of the money. You just go where it's best for you.' It's funny because I considered myself to be pretty powerful—I had a good job, I traveled around the country, I loved my family. It never dawned on me that I had never made life decisions based on what *I* wanted. I just figured I'd make myself happy wherever we ended up."

"Another day I'll never forget was August 26, 1992. We had moved to Indianapolis, Indiana, and were living in a hotel while we waited for our home to be vacated. Jim went off to work. As soon as I dropped the kids off at school, I went back to the hotel and lay down on the sofa and went to sleep for three years. I was so out of touch with my world that it was as if my rational mind had shut down. I couldn't tap into it. I had been such a dynamo all my life, but in this move, I lost the ability to plan, to create, to vision, to keep a big picture. All I could do was get through each day. I'd get up in the morning, take the kids to school, come back and lay on the sofa. Just before they came home for lunch, I'd get up, fix them lunch, and then go back to the sofa. This kept going on every day. I'd go to the kids' activities and come home and be exhausted. I had no words for it then, but now I know my self was demanding to be born.

"My soul seemed to need to take away everything in my life, except, thank God, my husband and boys, and it was demanding that I *choose* what to put back into my life. Then I started getting sick. My body was shutting down on me, too."

It wasn't until Nancy's father, a doctor, saw her and noticed how thin and haggard she had become that she realized she was severely depressed. She had begun to think about dying a lot and about all the diseases that might end her life. Receiving a respite with the antidepressant Prozac, she began to think more clearly. "I had two therapists who tried to help, but that was basically a disaster because they were trying to help me on merely the cognitive level—helping me to consider going back to graduate school, for example. But until I came upon Thomas Moore's book *The Care of the Soul,* I had no way of knowing that it was my soul that was sick. I didn't know where to go to get help for that. It felt like the pain of the universe was rushing through me. I had felt so lazy and undisciplined, lying on the sofa day after day, but I began to realize dimly that what I was feeling wasn't about character flaws.

"Eventually I was introduced to a wonderful therapist, Windy Wilson. One day I was describing to her a luncheon I had gone to where I had nothing to say to anyone. I had felt utterly bored. That's when she told me, 'Nancy, you are on the hero's journey.' I had no idea what that meant, but it resonated with me. I was not used to thinking about universal energy or being connected to the divine. But when she said that to me, I trusted her in my deepest being. She became my guide. She affirmed what I was doing. Since all I was doing was sitting on the sofa, she would say, 'Go home and sit on the sofa intentionally. You will know when it's time to get up.'

"I began reading voraciously. I intuitively got exactly the book I needed next. Or I'd buy a book and put it down. Six months later, I'd find it and wonder, 'Where was this all the time?' That taught me about timing. Windy kept telling me, 'You are not making mistakes.'

"During this time I felt there was no light in my life. I described it as being on the Dark Side of the Moon. I sat on the sofa for three to four years. It was the only way I could hear my own voice. Now I can see that I needed to learn to be quiet. It was the only way I could be taught that. I had had what I call the "crushing calendar" life. I had always kept myself so busy, I had no time to contemplate what I was doing. The move to Indianapolis caused me to get rid of anything that would stimulate me. There was no landscape, no activity, no interest in acquiring anything—all the things that used to take up my time. I tried to recreate my life by getting another position at the local branch of my old company, but I just couldn't do it. The only thing I had any energy for was going to the bookstore and being with my children."

What helped Nancy come through this difficult period of the void? "The biggest thing I did was trust that what I needed would come to me. I stopped trying to figure out what to do. I began to notice where my attention was being drawn—to women's issues, refugees, mothers, and babies. I began to have a gut sense that the energy in the world is out of balance. I began to pay attention to my dreams. I feel today that I have completely assimilated the ability to be patient. I have absolute trust that I'm being led to go where I need to go. My morning prayer is, 'Let me be of service.' It still is not clear to me what the next step or involvement is going to be, but I know now that I am being led to doing what's important at the level of my soul. I just don't know what form that's going to take."

Experiencing the Void

Let's review some of the points of Nancy's experience in the void:

- Her husband's layoff and their sudden move were signals that a new life was struggling to be born.
- The old, busy schedule of activities kept her from listening to the needs of her soul.
- She had never stopped long enough to find her own inner needs — her own soul's choices.
- With the help of her counselor, she entered the void (or sat on the couch) with intention.
- She realized the void came because she needed to learn to be quiet.
- She learned to trust that what she needed would come to her.
- She stopped trying to figure out what to do.
- She began to notice where her attention was being drawn.
- She began to pay attention to her dreams.
- She began to trust absolutely that she was being led to go where she needed to go for the requirements of her soul.

✔ Circle the insights that stood out the most for you.
✔ Make TIP CARDS on index cards for the insights you wish to have handy.
✔ If you like, record them as well on page 237 of the profile sheet.

WORKING THROUGH OBSTACLES

The way we imagine, describe, or feel our blocks can provide us a door into their solution. Part of learning to trust our intuition is learning the language of our intuition and how it speaks to us — in images, sounds, thought patterns, or specific ideas. We've all said at one time or another: *I've hit a wall. I'm drawing a blank. I can't see the forest for the trees. I'm under the gun. I'm stuck. The shit has really hit the fan. I can't see my way around this problem. There's no way out. I feel like I'm in a big hole and can't get out. I'm in the void.*

✔ If you are feeling a block or stymied by a problem, describe here your feelings about it or how you see it. _____

_____

_____

_____

_____

Quick Meditation for Working Through Obstacles

One liberating and creative way to work with blocked energy is to imagine it symbolically.

- Find a quiet place to sit or lie where you won't be disturbed for ten to fifteen minutes. Have a notebook and pen handy to help focus your questions and capture your answers.
- With eyes closed, take some deep, soft inhalations and let your body completely relax.
- After a few minutes, keeping your mood of relaxation and tranquillity, gently open your eyes and do the following:

1. *Describe your problem.* Write down here or in your notebook a specific description of your current problem. _____

_____

_____

_____

_____

2. *Feel it emotionally.* Describe your feelings about the problem.

_____

_____

_____

3. *Feel it physically.* Describe where these feelings are located in your body. _____

_____

_____

_____

4. *See it.* With eyes closed, visualize the shape, size, color, and texture of your problem.

5. *Hear it.* With eyes closed, listen for any sounds your problem makes.

6. *Find the gift within it.* With eyes closed, ask for a symbol to appear that represents the gift within the obstacle. Write down *everything* you see, hear, or imagine, even if you think you are "making it up." Don't analyze anything at this point. Just keep breathing, and close your eyes again. _____

_____

_____

_____

7. *Accept the fear you have about the obstacle.* Notice how the obstacle may keep you from facing another fear. Ask yourself: *If I didn't have this obstacle, what would I still be afraid of?* _____

_____

_____

_____

8. *What must you believe if you have this problem in your life?* Close your eyes and reflect on what *belief* underlies this obstacle. Write down anything that comes to mind. _____

_____

_____

_____

_____

9. *What is the message of the symbol?* Summarize the information you got from this meditation. _____

_____

_____

_____

_____

10. *What is a creative next step or solution?* Close your eyes again and ask this question. Notice what comes into your mind. An image? A message? A sound? Write down whatever came to you without judging it. You may understand it at a later time, or it may make perfect sense to you right now. _____

_____

_____

_____

_____

✔ What symbol emerged that represented a creative next step? Make a note on page 237 of your profile sheet.

Brother Cleopa

Brother Cleopa, an Orthodox monk who died at age eighty-seven, once fled Communist pressure by becoming an anchorite in Romania's forests. Born of illiterate parents in northern Romania, he entered the fourteenth-century Sihastra Monastery, two hundred miles north of Bucharest. As he cared for the monastery's sheep, he quickly gained respect within the religious community for his remarkable memory. "I met Brother Cleopa in between my prison terms," recalled the Reverend Roman Braga, a seventy-seven-year-old priest who spent eleven years in custody in Communist Romania. "I had heard of him and traveled to see him in the early 1950s. He was not highly educated, but he was able to speak in simple ways that were at the same time very deep and went to the heart of his listeners. He spoke of ordinary things but in ways that made you think of God. I remember how joyful he was. He kept saying that life was a gift, and he had his special way of greeting you; he would say, 'May Heaven consume you.'"

The monk was elected abbot of the monastery, and his reputation continued to spread. People began traveling to the remote monastery to seek his absolution and guidance. After the Communist Party took control of Romania, he was told to tell the people who were coming to see him to go away. "Instead," said Braga, "he left the monastery and became a hermit. He went into the mountain forests, living in solitude in an underground den he built. Woodsmen brought him sacks of potatoes each month, and every day he would eat one potato."

After Stalin died in 1953, pressure on the Orthodox Church eased, and Brother Cleopa was able to return to the monastery. His reputation for wisdom and good humor grew. He was invited to lecture at universities, and his sermons were published under the title "Talks with Brother Cleopa."[8] In the tradition of the order as a sign of respect, he was buried sitting upright on a stool.

CHAPTER 12

Where We Lose Power

If aspects of the person remain undigested—cut off, denied, projected, rejected, indulged, or otherwise unassimilated—they become the points around which the core forces of greed, hatred, and delusion attach themselves. They are black holes that absorb fear and create the defensive posture of the isolated self, unable to make satisfying contact with others or with the world.

—MARK EPSTEIN, M.D.[1]

Bob is one of my favorite clients. He has had it all, lost it all, and rebounded from a downward spiral to being truly in his element.

In his early forties, Bob founded an innovative product and built a company of international recognition. But his relationship with his partners eventually fell apart, and Bob moved on. The move cost him great financial losses, his marriage, and his vitality, which was further weakened by prostate problems. His self-confidence severely shaken, Bob halfheartedly developed a consulting business and fell into a thinly disguised major depression, which sapped his creative energy. Hounded by creditors, lawyers, and an irate ex-wife, and discouraged by a lack of cash flow, Bob tuned out the world by glibly denying the depth of his problems to friends and by answering only selected calls, which he screened with his answering machine. I could never reach Bob directly since his machine was always on.

BOB'S STORY

One day when we were talking, I asked Bob, "What would make you happy—besides a million dollars to pay off your debts?" Without much hesitation, he said, "You know, the only time I've really felt good about myself—felt alive—was when I was on the stage standing in front of others." Bob had studied acting and playwriting in college, and he sang and played the piano fairly well. "I feel my purpose in life is to stand in front of people and inspire them." From his quiet, dejected demeanor, it was obvious that Bob didn't think he had a chance in hell to do that at this stage of the game.

We talked some more. After some time, I reflected back to him some of my impressions of his situation. "First of all, Bob," I said, "You never answer the phone directly. You have barricaded yourself against any synchronistic event coming in to you over the phone. You're effectively cutting off your source of energy and contacts from the outside world." Although I knew the answer, I asked, "Why do you always have your call-screening on?" "Well, I get all these calls from creditors," he said. "I don't want to talk to them." I could certainly relate to that, since I, too, had suffered financial problems after my second divorce.

"Well, let's use the principle that your purpose is still attracting to you what you need. Who's been calling you?"

"MasterCard, Visa," he answered glumly.

"MasterCard and Visa, hmm?" I said. "Those are big companies, right?" He nodded, wondering where I was going with this.

"Why not try something new. Would you be willing to answer your phone directly one hour a day? Just pick up the phone and take your chances, for only one hour a day. How about it?" He still looked dubious, but nodded to humor me.

In my experience, creditors call because they want to keep track of you, and they want to know you intend to pay them. "So if you answer the phone, and it happens to be MasterCard," I said, "how about saying something like, 'You

> "As for the inner level of obstacle, perhaps nothing ever really attacks us except our own confusion. Perhaps there is no solid obstacle except our own need to protect ourselves from being touched. Maybe the only enemy is that we don't like the way reality is now and therefore wish it would go away fast. But what we find as practitioners is that nothing ever goes away until it has taught us what we need to know."
> —Pema Chodron[2]

know, I really want to pay your bill, but I need work in order to make the money to pay you. Since I'm a corporate trainer, is there anybody in your human resource department you can refer me to, to talk about training?' " Bob laughed for the first time in our conversation.

"Oh, God. That would be a joke, all right."

I asked him to put an index card next to his phone that said "Anything is possible" and to give it a try. A week later, Bob called and said, "I did it! I answered the phone and it was from MasterCard. I told the collection woman exactly what you said, and she burst out laughing! I didn't get any referrals for training out of it," Bob laughed, "but you know what? After that phone call I felt so much better about myself, it's like I kind of broke that trance I was in. I know I'm going to get back on my feet eventually. I feel like I've shifted something in myself."

Bob had been able to shift himself, using his inborn talent for making people laugh, to begin to break up some of the dense inner blocks he was putting up in front of every part of his life.

But this was only the beginning. I continued to meet with Bob, and using the principle that the universe is sending you what you need, even though it might not come in the package you expect, I asked, "So, Bob. Tell me again, what it is you want?"

"I want to be able to stand in front of people and inspire them."

We talked about how Bob had originally seen his life purpose as acting or singing when he was in his twenties. But now, who knows how that same goal might be achieved?

"Tell me who else is calling you," I prodded.

"Oh, I get dozens of "maybe" projects. Stuff that never pans out. I don't know. Well, yeah, there's one guy, Dean, that's been calling me."

Sensing something special about this Dean, I asked, "So who is Dean? What's he want? What's your take on him?"

"Oh, he works at [a big Silicon Valley company]. He does training for them, and he's been calling to talk to me about possibly doing something with him."

The very downcast way that Bob was talking somehow alerted my intuition, and I said, "Bob, this sounds like training work for you. Why are you not following up with Dean?"

"Well, I don't really like the guy all that much. And I think his training material is really outdated," he responded, but I could tell that he was already slightly reevaluating these calls from Dean, and so I said, "What's the real reason you didn't call him back?"

"Well, I really am not that crazy about him. But I think the real reason is that I didn't initiate this opportunity, so it doesn't feel real to me."

Now we were getting somewhere. We had discovered some beliefs Bob had about how he "had to make things happen" or they didn't count as real opportunities. Was this a guy thing? I wondered to myself.

"Well, Bob, this sounds like the universe handing you a blessing in disguise. This sounds like a chance to stand up in front of people and inspire them. You may have to do some work revamping the material, but that's exactly the kind of creative work that turns you on. Are you going to call him back?"

Bob really had no choice, the way I put it! To make a long story short, he did call Dean back, did begin to do some trainings with him, and now has successfully developed his own style and contacts and is very much on the upswing financially. Bob has found his niche, at least for now.

✔ What stood out for you in Bob's story? Jot down any insights here or on page 237 of the profile sheet.

_____

_____

_____

_____

SELF-ANALYSIS OF LIMITING PATTERNS OF BEHAVIOR

The following material is adapted from *The Purpose of Your Life*, pages 223–225. There are various ways that we sabotage our path, but life would be boring if it were predictable and easy. As we tumble about, lurching toward our goals, falling into our own pitfalls, struggling back up into the light, we learn major soul lessons—if we remain aware of what's happened.

Review the following patterns and see if any of these are familiar. This analysis might be useful to do with a good friend. Avoid doing the exercise with a family member unless you have a harmonious relationship and have never had major emotional conflicts with that person. It's also a good idea not to discuss these patterns with people you work with.

Lack of Good Judgment

Do I jump into friendship or intimacy too fast and then get scared and pull back? When I commit too soon, does it make me feel trapped, causing me to "back out" of things? Do I overlook obvious signs of future trouble with a company because I am so desperate to take any job? Do I listen to my instincts about a prospective boss or company? Do I fail to state clearly to myself what it is that I value and want to have in my life?

✔ How can I become more aware of the "red flag" when I'm about to make a decision without giving myself adequate time or facts to evaluate what I want to do?

✔ Am I willing to slow down? Am I willing to honor myself enough not to make hasty commitments?

✔ What affirmation could I make to allow myself to believe that I do have good judgment?

Overaccommodating and People-Pleasing

Do I always try to please everybody by using many different personas? Am I flattering, overly rational and businesslike, flirtatious, cynical, too nice, or too accommodating? Do I exhibit any other behavior that is motivated by the desire to "be chosen?" Do I say one thing to my coworkers and then talk about them behind their back to others? Do I feel appeasement is the best way to feel in control?

✔ How can I stay more in integrity in situations in which I think I need other people to like me?

✔ Will I remember to feel the sensations in my body when I am around others?

✔ Can I begin to feel the inner power that comes from accepting who I am, just as I am?

Craving Recognition

Do I have a pattern of wanting recognition for everything I do? Am I doing something because I get lots of money or recognition, rather than doing something I enjoy? Do I try to ingratiate myself with the boss because she is in the power position?

✔ Can I begin to feel the inner power that comes from accepting who I am, just as I am?

✔ What anonymous service can I perform that will make me feel good even if I don't get credit for it?

✔ How can I do my job even better, just for the joy of knowing I'm committed to excellence for its own sake?

Talking Too Much

Do I have to control the conversation or take center stage by incessantly talking or talking about myself? When I notice people distancing themselves from me, do I try to keep talking faster to keep the connection going? Is it difficult for me to listen? Do I frequently interrupt business meetings with jokes or silliness?

✔ Do I see where this pattern came from? (Being the baby of the family? Being the entertainer of the family to avoid or camouflage tensions and conflict?)

✔ Am I in touch with my feelings when I know I'm starting to overtalk?

Suspicion and Secretiveness

Do I feel I must keep certain ideas to myself so others won't steal them or beat me to the punch? How does my suspicion keep me from gaining support (e.g., on a project) when I need it?

✔ How *specifically* do I distance myself from others?

✔ What *specifically* about someone makes me become distrustful?

✔ How can I practice being more open with others? What makes me feel safe?

Withholding Love

Do I use silence or smoldering, unexpressed anger to let people know that I am upset, without giving them a chance to talk it through with me? What subtle forms of withholding energy do I use in the workplace?

✔ How can I practice accepting and receiving from others in a gracious way?

✔ How can I begin to participate more in my life?

Resisting Authority and Cynicism

Do I tend to become elated only when I have made someone else feel inadequate or wrong? Do I see myself as a lone ranger or the only one who sees "the truth" in a situation, even though I rarely do anything constructive to change anything? What specifically do I feel when I have one-upped someone? How has this sabotaged my progress in the past when I wanted to succeed?

✔ How can I be kinder and gentler? Why would I want to do that?

Self-Righteousness

Do I feel most powerful right after I have been "proven right" in a situation? Is it inordinately important for me to be right all the time? Is it very hard, or impossible, for me to admit any oversight or misjudgment?

✔ Could I possibly say "I'm sorry" even once this week?
✔ How can I begin to back off a little bit and relax?
✔ Do I need to make everybody else wrong to feel good about myself?
✔ What else do I have to offer besides criticism?

Unwillingness to Commit

What does commitment mean to me? What do I think I have to give up to be committed to something? Does remaining uncommitted make me feel more secure, *because then I always have open-ended options?* What specifically do I feel when I have lots of options? Am I addicted to the *potential* of a career, job, or project? Am I always waiting for that big break or that big client? If I hate my work, do I secretly set myself apart from my colleagues because I believe this is not my "real" work?

✔ Is there any small step I can promise to take this week? How does that commitment make me feel?

Commitment to Something That Will Never Work

Do I believe that I have to struggle to make something work even when I am getting every sign to let it go? Do I work marathon hours or take less money than I am worth?

✔ What is my top priority? Am I likely to achieve that?
✔ Is there something else I'd rather be doing?

Always Thinking There Is Something Better Than What You Have

Are you always fixated on some golden future that never comes? Do you take small steps toward your goals or give up because your goal seems too big and impossible? Are you chronically dissatisfied and constantly letting everyone know it? Can you truthfully acknowledge your strengths and achievements?

✔ How can you have a little more fun and satisfaction tomorrow?

Automatically Assuming Your Needs Will Be Met by the Other

Do you bring your needs and childhood lacks to an intimate relationship instead of your strength, kindness, and openness to learn about the other person? Do you expect that people can read your mind and provide everything you desire when you desire it?

✔ If you need help with communication, are you willing to find a good therapist?

When Things Get Tough, You Get Going

If a circumstance doesn't satisfy you, do you check out? Do you decide everything is wrong with your workplace the minute things get difficult or if you get a new boss you don't like?

✔ What is the real truth about what you want?

_____
_____
_____
_____
_____
_____
_____

"Habituation, then, is the by-product of all the routines, ruts and pigeonholing that our minds have indulged in for decades. By midlife, this mechanism becomes predominant in us, censoring, categorizing, distorting, judging, assuming, routinizing, mechanizing everything we seek, feel, and think. Habituation sets in, for example, when we no longer hear what people are saying to us (because our preconceived notions tell us we know the truth already). . . . It is, in short, a reduction of our awareness rather than an expansion of our consciousness."

—Harry R. Moody[3]

✔ Have you tried being truthful in a situation and letting the truth change the situation, rather than leaving before you've participated honestly with others?

Fear of Change

When you reach a new level of responsibility or recognition, do you fear that you won't be able to maintain it? Do you dig your feet in against taking any action until you have "complete clarity" about what will happen?

✔ *Feel the fear.* Talk to the fear; ask what is the worst thing the fear thinks will happen.

✔ *Take a small positive step toward something that makes you happy.* Ask your fear if it can suggest something small that would be helpful to do right now. Ask the fear what it would like to have in order to move ahead.

✔ *Ask for help.* If you face something difficult, how can you have someone on your side to help you in any way?

UNRAVELING THE PATTERN

- If you resonate to one or two of these patterns, write down your insights on an index card. Keep the card where you can see it, and let it remind you of the work you are doing to release your attachment to this unproductive behavior.
- Without judging yourself, make a clear intention to work on making better choices in the future.
- Ask to be given opportunities to heal these patterns. Remember, change doesn't always happen overnight. You have been coping with life by using these patterns. They have been a big part of your complex nature, and they have also contributed to your uniqueness.
- Try to avoid taking the stance that these patterns are awful or that they make you a bad person. Judgments against yourself merely feed your shadow (the place where you store criticisms and feelings of inadequacy). Use these patterns to observe yourself and learn how they might lead to new choices. From a spiritual point of view, working with these patterns may be an important part of your life purpose! In any case, becoming aware of them engages your soul's purpose for spiritual awakening.

BREAKING UP THE PATTERN:
FIVE-MINUTE WRITING EXERCISE

To gain more awareness, take one of the preceding patterns that you recognize in yourself, and write without lifting the pen from the paper for five minutes (with your timer set). Start with one question, and write as if you are answering your question.

For example, let's say your pattern is self-righteousness. Ask yourself, "What am I afraid will happen if I am shown to be wrong about something? Think back to a childhood memory of a time when you made a mistake. What were the attitudes of your parents, teachers, and peers toward making a mistake? Do you blame others for your problems? If so, you will keep creating power struggles all your life. Because you learned in childhood that making mistakes resulted in losing love or security, you pushed your fear of being wrong into the shadow. Thus, the need to blame others may seem vital to fend off the anxiety of making a mistake. To grow beyond this fear, you eventually have to realize that you can make a mistake and "not die"—as you feared as a child.

If your pattern is overtalking, ask yourself, "How would I feel if no one in the room spoke for ten minutes? What about silence makes me afraid?" The next time you are in a meeting, practice being quiet and feeling what this tension feels like in your body. Later, when you have time, remember these bodily sensations and write about them as if they were "voices" speaking to you.

In the next week, begin to notice how you get angry at yourself for certain things. Notice how often you talk to yourself negatively. Try to see how you are spending your precious life energy in ways that are not nourishing your life purpose. Simply becoming aware of this self-bombardment will help you to reclaim your power; however, you may want to work on these patterns with a therapist to deepen the process.

THE MIRROR EXERCISE

Is there someone in your life who really bugs you? Why? In the space that follows, list all the things you don't like about him or her. Be specific. When you are done, forget about the exercise—don't look at it for at least twenty-four hours. When you have time, go back and insert your name wherever you have used the other person's name. Now, can you see any of the other person's faults in yourself, even in small ways? Seeing the same traits in yourself as you see so vividly in others is useful because it takes you out of being a victim of these so-called horrible people and gives you compassion and humility. These negative traits are not something to berate yourself for but serve as reminders of tender places in you that need healing. _____

_____

_____

_____

ARE YOU LOSING POWER IN THE WORKPLACE?

Answer the following questions to determine how much power you lose on a daily basis while on the job. Determine the percentage of time you spend on each of the following items every day and add it all up. Let's assume you have "100 percent energy" when you wake up. As you spend that energy in the following negative thought forms, you are being depleted of that energy. Notice how your initial 100 percent drops. The remainder is what's left to use doing the job you were hired to do. The five steps on pages 177–178 will help you to change your attitudes and actions.

Power Loss Analysis

1. How much energy do you invest in taking on other people's issues and conflicts? With whom are you doing this right now?

_____

_____

2. How often do you feel pressure to perform to appease your boss or coworkers instead of doing what you know is right? Can you remember a time when you agreed to something that was out of alignment with what you knew to be true? _____

_____

_____

3. How often do you find yourself stewing about unfair policies and procedures? What policies are you most upset about right now?

_____

_____

What would you like to do about it? _____
_____

What's stopping you? _____
_____

Whatever is stopping you is a belief you have (probably since childhood in some form or another).

4. How much time and energy do you spend thinking of revenge
against someone who has wronged you or stolen your thunder?
_____
_____

5. How much time each day do you spend focusing on negative
self-judgment? _____
_____

6. How much time do you find yourself regretting your failures?
Describe one failure. What was the most positive thing you can say
about it? _____
_____
_____

7. How much time do you spend relishing resentments toward
others? Does focusing on others' rottenness and talking about it a lot
make you feel better or more resentful? _____
_____

8. How much of your day is spent sending negative energy to your
enemies (this includes gossip, unpleasant thoughts, and small belittle-
ments)? _____
_____

9. How much energy do you spend trying to control others or con-
vince them that your point of view is the correct one? _____
_____

10. How much energy do you spend worrying about how well your
ideas are received, what others think of you, missing deadlines, or not
being able to accomplish your goals? _____
_____

How to Let Go of the Daily Frustrations and Drain

1. Remember your place in the big picture. If you're part of a
   group, what is your group trying to accomplish? What is your
   organization's best and worst contribution to the world? Can
   you let go of some grievance that isn't that important right now?

2. Ask yourself, "Does this [policy, goal, task] go against my principles?" If it does, can you find a way to reframe the goal into something you feel good about doing? If you can, take full responsibility for making it work. If you can't, begin to explore other options that are more in alignment with your beliefs and values.

3. Every time you find yourself thinking of revenge, stop. Take a deep breath. Remind yourself that this bitterness is draining *you*. Is it worth it to spend your valuable time and energy in this manner? Call back your energy. Practice feeling neutral about the person, or find something positive about him or her. However, don't force a feeling of phony good will.

4. If you're up against an obstacle, frustration, or delay, assume there is a purpose for it. Ask yourself, "How do I need to change my thinking or my attitude? Do I need to rethink my goal?" At a later time, the obstruction may be seen as a blessing.

5. How can you make the best of the situation you're in right now? One way is to consider the higher purpose for which this group was formed. Don't focus on a petty grievance as a way to feel superior in circumstances that may make you feel, deep down, resentful and helpless. Satisfaction in working with others will not come from trying to change them. The best way to work with a group is to decide that you are going to participate in the best way you can. And by doing so you will set an example that will raise the energy and vision for the whole group. This goal will put you squarely into the flow of your life purpose, because your life purpose is not what you do but who you are.

✔ What insights do you wish to record here? _____
_____
_____
_____

MARY'S STORY: COMING FULL CIRCLE

Mary became an insurance agent on the Monday after her father's death on Friday afternoon. "My father had been with his company for thirty years. When he died, I took over his business out of a sense of loyalty more than from a desire to do that career." Mary took to her job with enthusiasm. However, it soon became evident that her company was not about to reciprocate in its loyalty to Mary and her family. The situation began to deteriorate after she suffered some business losses during her first pregnancy. During her second pregnancy, she went into preterm labor owing to the stress and fear of being let go: Her company threatened to fire her because her sales were down. "California employers are supposed to accommodate women during pregnancy, which

> "In my understanding of Tibetan teachings, they believe that we always exist and work with forces that have already been set in motion. Since we can have little effect on those past thoughts and decisions, the most we can hope to do in every present moment is to add positive energy."
> —Conversation with Bill Fannin, doctor of Chinese medicine, Petaluma, California

means they won't terminate you if your sales are down. There was a technicality in my employment contract which meant that I was outside that protection. Two years later, during the first three months of my third pregnancy, they threatened to terminate me again, which caused me so much fear about losing all that I had accomplished in my career that I lost the baby. That started a cycle of fear and six months of depression. I didn't rebound for a year. During that time there were several so-called accidents in policy administration at my work, like dropping my securities license. They lost all my miscarriage medical claims. There was a palpable lack of support.

"Because of all I went through, I began to feel it was part of my life purpose to fight these kinds of policies for women in the future. I carried this anger and fear in my heart for years almost as a way to protect myself.

"Two weeks ago, the mediation date finally came, and I was terrified at confronting lawyers for the agency. Just before the meeting, I had two panic attacks.

"The week before the mediation, I saw your book [*The Purpose of Your Life*], and I thought, 'This is perfect.' I had no idea where I was going. I had worked in insurance my whole adult life, and I didn't know what I was going to do next. I saw your class on the web page. At that moment I received a commission check for the exact amount of the class, and my husband agreed to baby-sit the kids! I just laughed at the synchronicity.

"After the class I realized that it was not my life purpose to be Joan of Arc in this battle to the bitter end. Maybe it was enough just to have brought it this far and to have stimulated these questions of employee rights at the company. I realized I don't want to live in this fear and pain and anger anymore. I got a very strong feeling of joy. I felt there was a strong possibility that the mediation would end satisfactorily, and I told this to my husband, who is a lawyer. He told me, 'Well, don't get your hopes up. It probably won't be ended.' I brought some angel cards with me to the meeting. (I picked the words openness, light, grace.) I said several prayers.

"I was able to go in to the meeting with peace in my heart and really listen to the mediator. Even the lawyers were nicer than I expected. Everything worked out. Even though I was awarded less money than I asked for, I felt satisfied, and more importantly, I could now let go of it all.

"An odd thing happened at the end of the meeting. As we sat signing the final document, I turned around to get breathing room, and I saw the exact same building where I had first moved when my dad died! It was where it all started. Full circle. It was an exquisite moment. For two years I hadn't even been able to go downtown into the financial district because I would get panic attacks. Now, all my agony was over. It was a very meaningful moment for me.

"Now I think my life purpose is about story telling—redemptive stories of people going through things normal to human experience, but from which we turn away, such as difficult childhoods, child abuse, loneliness, and injustice. I want to show the human side. I feel absolutely on purpose when I'm writing."

✔ What touched you about Mary's story? If you wish, record any insights here and on page 238 of the profile sheet.

_____

_____

_____

PART FIVE

BEING IT, DOING IT

CHAPTER 13

Creating the Magic Magnetic Circle

"If I wait until I am enlightened, I don't know when I can help," [Sister Chan Khong, a Vietnamese nun,] *said cheerfully. "So I decided to do that small work. I went to the slums alone. I helped the children with all my heart, and slowly I moved the hearts of many people around me."*

—China Galland[1]

CREATE A SUPPORT CIRCLE

Do you long for people to talk to about what's really important to you? Do you wish you had someone with whom you could talk over an important decision or brainstorm the steps toward a goal or dream?

One of the healthiest and most energizing things we can do for ourselves is to create a circle of people with whom we share our spiritual aspirations, questions, and progress. Research has shown, for example, that patients with cancer live longer if they participate in a support group.

If you wish you had a group, maybe it's up to *you* to be the magnet for this circle to come together. Remember our daily mantra "Today I want to meet good people"? Infuse that mantra with the intention to draw together like-minded people for a weekly meeting.

One of the best ways to develop the mind, body, and spiritual consciousness is to participate in long-term practice, either by yourself or, even better, with a group. An excellent guidebook for such integrated practice is *The Life We Are Given: A Long-Term Program for Realizing the Potential of Body, Mind, Heart, and Soul,* by George Leonard and

Michael Murphy, from which we excerpted the exercise called Take the Hit in Chapter 11.

Guidelines for Your Life Purpose Study Group

Here are some guidelines you might keep in mind as you begin "accidentally" to meet others who yearn for community. You need not fear that you are not "experienced" enough or knowledgeable enough to start a group. Your desire for support is enough. If your desire is strong, then most likely starting a group is an integral part of your purpose right now.

Talk to people.

When meeting others, listen intuitively if you feel drawn to ask them to join your group. Bring up the subject in conversation and see how they respond. You only need two or three others to start.

Set your meeting time.

Once you have your group, set some guidelines. Continuity is important in group work. People are more likely to be dependable if there is a consistent meeting time. Commit to a length of time that gives you a chance to bond, work together, and establish rapport. Once a week for two or three months is a good start.

Share the duties.

Who likes to do what? Either rotate the duties of facilitator, timekeeper, bringer of music, and meditation or ritual leader, or let each person be responsible for the part he or she likes to do.

Write a purpose statement for the group.

In the first session, discuss what it is that you each want from the group. What is the purpose of getting together? It's a good idea to have a flip chart or white board for writing down ideas, goals, feelings, and expectations. Keep refining the purpose statement with exactly the words that give people energy. Once people start laughing and feeling good about the exact words chosen, see if you can come up with one good group statement, such as "We're going with the flow to where we need to go!"

Commit to the group.
Be sure to discuss at the first meeting such ground rules as calling if you're not coming, showing up on time, and taking turns speaking. If you decide to let each person have five minutes for a quick check-in at the beginning of the meeting, people who are shy will know they are assured of having a chance to speak. Decide how you want to handle people who take up too much time and whether or how you will admit new members. Addressing these issues in the beginning will save you confusion and stress later on. Remember, what you bring to the group represents what you bring to life.

Speak the truth and listen with love.
These two actions are among the most powerful that you can bring to your group. There is no one right way to do anything. Be kind, be open, and resist the temptation to give advice. In Native American talking circles, a talking stick is passed from person to person, and only the person holding the stick speaks, while everyone else listens. You can use this method for part of the meeting by choosing an object to pass around.

Be adventurous.
Let inspiration suggest other places to hold your meetings. For example, stay alert for bookstore lectures that would be interesting as food for thought, or do a potluck once in a while (but make sure this does not become a burden that takes away from your discussion time).

Suggested Process for Your Study Group

First Meeting
- ✔ Sit in a circle. Circles create a powerful, healing, democratic energy.
- ✔ Go around the circle letting each person introduce him- or herself and give a brief reason for joining the group.
- ✔ Sharing a few synchronicities always helps the process of getting to know one another.
- ✔ As a group, go through the table of contents of this workbook and circle or highlight the exercises, points, and information you'd like to cover. Estimate how many meetings it might take to cover the topics. Ask members how many meetings they can commit to.

✔ Emphasize having fun. Don't get too serious, but do set your ground rules as noted previously.

✔ Pass around a roster, and delegate someone to type it up and distribute it at the next meeting.

✔ Agree to call the host or hostess of the next meeting if you are not going to be there or are going to be late. Waiting for someone to show up is a drain on the group energy.

Subsequent Meetings

✔ *Honor commitments.* If you agree to do homework during the week, be sure to follow through and bring your work to the next meeting. However, be open to a change in topic if someone has "taken a hit" during the week and needs to process something.

✔ *Start with a meditation.* A good way to start a meeting is to have someone lead a simple guided meditation. After members have jotted down their impressions from the meditation, have everyone draw one of the oracle cards (see Chapter 10, this volume.) Then, go around the circle and let all persons speak about what is in their heart in the moment—either what they got in their meditation, the symbolic meaning they attribute to their oracle card, or something noteworthy that happened that week.

✔ *Handle intimidators and "poor me's."* It is not at all unusual to have group members who talk more than their share or who tend to fall into a "poor me" type of storytelling. It will be obvious that this is happening because suddenly the energy in the group will drop lower and lower. It is important for each member of the group to stay attuned to energy fluctuations. If a person is going on and on in a negative way that doesn't seem to go anywhere, someone needs to mention kindly that the energy seems to be getting stuck and suggest that the speaker needs to move on. Try not to accuse the person of being a "victim," but don't sit in silence when you know that nothing is going to be gained from a rambling account of troubles. When one person dominates a group, it erodes the coherence of the group. People simply won't want to keep coming.

Instead of getting fed up and dropping out, decide how you want to share your feelings about what is happening without blaming anyone. You can always say, "When you are talking, I feel drained and somewhat guilty, like I should come up with a solution to the problem. Is there some way you want this group to help you?" The person then has the option of asking for something directly and may even gain an insight about his or her disruptive pattern. In response to overtalking, you might say, "I'm noticing that some of us are not getting equal time to share. How would people feel about having a timekeeper to keep things moving?"

✔ *Resist the temptation to give advice.* Active listening to a speaker's feelings is always appropriate. Don't try to jump immediately to a solution. Gradually, as your sharing unfolds deeper layers, it will become obvious to the person what needs to be done. When someone is confused and downcast, it may be appropriate to ask, "What do you think you need to do?" Gently remind everyone that they have all come to learn new ways of expressing their purpose in life and to recognize and release old patterns. Be kind, but be direct without being judgmental—a good lesson for everyone!

✔ *Keep a record of synchronicities or answers to prayers.* Track what members attract into their lives by using the master attracting meditation on pages 111–112.

✔ Be creative. Be open. Have fun. Stay relaxed!

CHAPTER 14

Making a Difference

If you look back over your life. . . . you'll probably notice there's a vast gray sea of recollection, and embedded in it are a few crystal clear moments of vivid memories . . . [that] share something in common, and that something is at the core of the meditative state: it's what I call presence.

—THOM HARTMANN[1]

In the coming days, each of us will be faced with many new decisions. No longer does it seem possible to take for granted the life we have been living.

As your desire for clarity, security, and meaning—a way to make a difference in the world—grows from your inborn life purpose, you will be attracted to arenas that may be presently invisible to you. Wherever you find yourself presently has a purpose. Conditions are now being laid for further developments. It's important to remember that the emergence of your life purpose requires necessary and specific conditions. The fact that you have been moved to work with the principles in this book is a sign that you are part of the planetary plan and are being called to come forward.

More will be revealed each day as you listen to your intuition and notice the kind of people to whom you are attracted. I have selected the following stories to demonstrate the power of individual awareness coming into action. Read them with an open mind, and see what, if anything, speaks to you concerning your own path. In particular, notice the various settings in which the modern heroes of these stories play out their life scripts.

SAVING THE VILLAGE

"There was a loss of pride," said Maria Lastenia Pito, a weaver and vice governor of the governing council of Pitayo, Colombia, a reservation that had begun growing opium under pressure from drug traffickers. "The whole community was falling apart." Pito, founder of a cooperative of weavers, saw the effect easy drug money was having on every aspect of village life. For a community whose economy had been based on barter, the influx of excess money tore the heart out of the delicate balance of the social system. Consumerism, drug-related violence, and alcoholism, as well as the insidious loss of authority within the family, wreaked havoc at every level. The entire culture was on the verge of disappearing. Pito took action, and launched a campaign to eradicate the poppy plant. Despite resistance to her because she is a woman, last October the farmers agreed to destroy 865 acres of poppies and return to self-sufficiency by growing traditional, legal crops such as potatoes, corn, wheat, and onions. The village of Pitayo has become a role model, and the U.S. government recently agreed to finance "alternative development" programs to help coca and poppy growers switch to legal crops, which has proved to be a far more effective approach than aggressive, military-assisted aerial fumigation.[2]

SAVING THE TURTLES

For almost twenty years, Maria Angela Marcovaldi and her husband, Guy, have been protecting the habitat and hatchlings of five of the world's eight species of marine turtles that migrate each year to Brazil's Atlantic coastline. In 1980 they began the TAMAR Project, a Portuguese acronym for marine turtles (*tartaruga marinha*). Two years before, they had both witnessed fishermen slitting the throats and stomachs of female turtles, staining the beach red. "I felt sick to my stomach," Guy recalled. "It was then that the idea for TAMAR was born." As a result, the Marcovaldis set out to prove to Brazilian fishermen that turtles were worth more alive than dead. "You can't expect people to die of hunger to save the environment," said Maria Angela.

They began by photographing the slaughter of the turtles, which caused a public outcry when the pictures were published in a leading newsmagazine. Leading a scientific survey of the sea turtles sponsored

> "Businesses are moving beyond the 'service' economy and into the 'experience' economy. Customers increasingly demand to have a unique experience in stores, such as a whole birthday party at a place like the Discovery Zone, rather than just buying a birthday cake from a bakery."
>
> —*The Futurist*[3]

by the government, the Marcovaldis and three colleagues gathered proof of the nesting sites on Brazilian beaches. Today, because of the work of TAMAR, the local people have an alternate livelihood based on ecotourism. The town, which receives three hundred thousand tourists a year, has a visitor's center, two open-air hatcheries, five display tanks, a museum, and gift shops stocked by the handiwork of local artisans. TAMAR biologists have introduced marine conservation to the high school curricula in two state capitals. Plans are afoot for a $5 million mini–sea world, whose revenue would be used for the project. Meanwhile, local children between eight and thirteen years are trained as "miniguides" and paid a monthly stipend. "The turtles were disappearing so fast, we hired the older generation who were killing and poaching, and then began educating the younger generation," said Guy in an interview.[4]

SOMETHING ELSE

A writer, composer, poet, and artist, Dick Higgins was known for works with titles such as "foew&ombwhnw," an acronym for "freaked out electronic wizard and other marvelous bartenders who have no wings." An influential figure in the avant-garde movement of the early 1960s, he also founded, funded, and ran several publishing companies, including Something Else Press, which published works by Gertrude Stein, Merce Cunningham, and John Cage. He was the cofounder of the Fluxus movement, which accepted any activity as art.

DOING WHAT MATTERS IN THE ENVIRONMENT

In 1998, at the age of eighty-six, David Brower, dean of America's conservation movement, won the Blue Planet Prize, the world's most lucrative environmental award. Brower said he plans to invest the prize, worth an estimated $427,600, in a fund that will provide "little seed grants" to environmental projects "that need help to get things going."

Brower, who was the first executive director of the Sierra Club, has been instrumental in creating nine national parks, keeping dams out of the Grand Canyon, and establishing the national wilderness system. Aggressive and un-compromising in political battles, he was forced to resign from the Sierra Club in 1969 but went on to found Friends of the Earth, the League of Conservation Voters, and Earth Island Institute. A col-lege dropout, Brower has received ten honorary university degrees, as well as awards from other environmental orga-nizations, and he has been nominated for the Nobel Prize.

> "When you ask people what paper is made from, most answer 'trees.' Actually, paper is made from cellulose fiber that can come from plants or trees. . . . Making paper from plant fiber instead of trees seems radical to some folks. To us it seems like the most natural thing in the world. The challenge is to get a larger portion of the population to be aware of this option and the obvious environmental and economic benefits it carries. One of the stumbling blocks in this effort is the way certain concepts are imbedded in our culture and government."
> —Newsletter from *Vision Paper*, makers of kenaf, a plant-fiber paper

OCEAN'S STORY

Ocean Robbins, son of author John Robbins, was fifteen when he decided to do something about the world in which he lived. "That year I attended a program on the environment where I met Ryan Eliason, who was then eighteen. We both wanted to do something to empower people our age to start making better choices that would affect the future." Now twenty-five, Robbins is the cofounder and president of Youth for Environmental Sanity (YES!) and author of *Choices for Our Future: A Generation Rising for Life on Earth*.

Becoming Active

"At YES! we work to help people make the transition from feeling like helpless victims of a mess they didn't create to active participants in the transformation of our world," Robbins said. "So often we don't see that we are collectively determining the future of life on earth. Every choice we make has an impact. The question is no longer 'Do I make a difference?' but 'What kind of a difference am I going to make?' "

DOES YOUR LIFE PURPOSE INCLUDE GARDENING OR TEACHING ABOUT GARDENING AND NUTRITION?

From Giorgio Cerquetti, *The Vegetarian Revolution*[5]

"Twenty vegetarians can be fed on the amount of land needed to feed one person consuming a meat-based diet.

"Reducing meat production in the U.S. by just ten percent would release enough grain to feed sixty million people."

—Jean Mayer, Harvard, nutritionist

"The petroleum used in the United States would decrease by 60% if people adopted a vegetarian diet.

"During World War II, many Americans planted 'victory gardens.' These gardens supplied families with food at a crucial point in our national history. Though not in the midst of a world war, we still need victory gardens: this time, to combat the environmental crisis and regenerate the earth."

—*The Green Lifestyle Handbook*

"People all over America will have very little choice but to become more vegetarian initially . . . and then totally vegetarian."

—Faith Popcorn, corporate trend-spotter

YES! Camps

"We run environmental training camps from one to three weeks long for high school–and college-age students. So far we've done forty-three sessions in seven countries. These camps help young people turn their concern into concrete action. Many young people who care about the world and the future tend to feel alone and isolated. The truth is we are never alone. There are people all over the planet actively working to bring their lives into alignment with their values. Our goal at YES! camps is to foster deeper connections with the natural world and with each other. We want to provide emotional and spiritual support, as well as effective tools, so that people can live their own life purposes.

"I've always cared about people and the world. As long as I can remember, I've felt that my life purpose was to be of service. The question I ask myself each day is, 'How can I be of the best service today to the people I care about, to humanity, to the future?' I feel most effective when I am helping others to live their purpose. So many people feel lost, and our society is full of distractions from what is really going on."

Starting Where You Are

"Ryan and I started YES! together in the garage. Our first project was to speak to high school and junior assemblies about the environment and about living your purpose. These talks evolved into the YES! tour. We reached five hundred ninety thousand students in about twelve hundred high schools and assemblies. We still do some touring, but now we speak more often at conferences.

"We've also shifted our focus to the camps—we do about ten every summer—because we can go so much deeper in a week than in an hour's lecture. We receive e-mail and letters and calls from past camp participants about how it changed their life and how they're carrying it forward, for example, by starting environmental clubs, recycling, becoming politically active, and becoming vegetarians and eating organic food. They also report improved relationships with friends and family, improved academic performance, and shifts in their career goals to be more in alignment with their values. After our programs, these young people are more aware of what's important to them, which helps them focus on more enlightened career goals, rather than just living out their parents' goals. They become motivated by their values and the desire to make a difference, not because somebody is telling them to do something.

"My work is to help people look at their lives and their world and ask themselves, 'What can I do to move a little closer to where I would like to be?' We have to be willing to be stretched to see at once the painful reality of how things are in the world and the awesome beauty of how they could be. We have to dare to bring our lives into alignment.

> "The students who showed the most significant immunological elevation were those who responded most positively to the notion of doing good for other people without being overly concerned with the results of their actions. Unwittingly, McClelland had discovered an actual physiological benefit that results both from doing good in the world, and from being in the world but not of it; that is, being in a state of detachment where, in McClelland's words, 'the person is not invested in the outcome of the thing—the person is not fixated on the goal of the activity.' "
> —Harry R. Moody[6]

Doing What Comes Naturally—and Doing It Positively

"People are not making changes in their lifestyle because they are martyrs. For example, if we associate the concept of consuming less with being less happy, we won't do it. But if we perceive consuming less as giving us a healthier lifestyle and increased self-esteem, then those changes will usually become permanent. Part of our work is to help people feel their connection to the natural world. Then they naturally want to do the right thing.

"At YES! we talk about being conscious of our individual life purposes and how each aware person is very much needed. For example, one person may see a problem and say, 'Oh, no, there's another reason it's hopeless!' We want people to say, "Another problem? Then here's another way I can be useful.' We believe that the pain we feel in response to a problem is a resource to motivate us to take action.

"There is a revolution taking place right now among young people. They are tired of being labeled by adults as apathetic and lost. Adults may say young people don't care, but the reality is they care a lot. They care so much that it hurts unless they can do something with that caring. But today more and more young people are realizing the power of their actions, taking responsibility for their lives, and creating profound positive changes in their schools, their communities, and ultimately in our global community."

If part of your life purpose resonates with the work these young people are doing, contact them and see how you can get involved. For information on speakers for high school programs or attending environmental summer camps or for copies of Robbins's book, *Choices for Our Future*, or of the video, *Connect*, which aired on MTV in 1997, contact Robbins and Eliason at their toll-free number (877) 2YESCAMP (877-293-7226). They are located at 420 Bronco Road, Soquel, CA 95073-9510. Send e-mail to camps@yesworld.org, or visit their website at www.yesworld.org.

THE FOURTH RIVER

Zenobia Barlow, a longtime friend and sister in the spiritual quest, has traveled the world from Texas to Mt. Kailas in Tibet—and just about all points in between. Her life purpose has unfolded through following her intuition, developing her passions, and stepping into the void.

Today she is the executive director of the Center for Ecoliteracy, in Berkeley, California.

When she first joined the group, it was a think tank founded by systems theorist, Fritjof Capra, best known for his books *The Tao of Physics* and *The Web of Life*. The center is now a foundation that supports education reform and other evolutionary projects. Members of the board include such visionary thinkers as Capra; environmental writer and educator David Orr; philanthropist Peter Buckley; Gaye Hoagland, a college professor and former director of the Regional Coalition for Essential Schools; and Barlow.

In a recent chat in her home office, surrounded by Chinese antique tables, comfortable rattan chairs, a myriad of photographs depicting altars and ceremonies around the world, and sitting next to a canary named Amarillo, Barlow described some of the turning points that led her to do work that matters deeply to her in each stage of her widely diverse life experiences.

Early Development of Intuition and Ability to Read Nonverbal Cues

"I've always lived what seems like parallel existences—an immersion in both the inner and outer worlds. I think my inner-directed experiences started simply because I was so very nearsighted when I was a child growing up in Texas. I didn't even know I was nearsighted until I was about twelve. Up to then I would say I lived with a defocused frame of reference. Because I lacked so many details in my vision, I early on saw life in terms of patterns and composition. To be intuitive I think sometimes you need to defocus your attention and tune into another level.

"At the same time, growing up on a nine thousand-acre working ranch and being close to the earth, I've always been adept at getting things done in the real world, too. The parallel existences for me are like two different zones: One zone is where I am observing unspoken or intangible relationships between the amazing diversity of people with whom I work. Or where I am observing how theoretical ideas underlie practical systems or even making artistic decisions in my photography or for our publications. That all seems to come out of the intuitive realm. The rest of the time, I am very practical and productive. It feels a little like a figure eight, where my inner processes direct my choices in the outside world of things, and then I go back inside for the next cycle."

Barlow continued to describe the development of her intuition as a young girl of eleven herding cattle in blizzards alongside seasoned ranch hands. "I would get up before dawn, and the first thing I had to do was catch a horse. I've learned some things from catching a horse that I've used all my life. For one thing, you can't move directly toward it. You must approach the animal quietly and slowly and peripherally to allow it to get used to you. The shortest distance between the two of you is not necessarily a straight line. Fritjof Capra talks about this phenomenon as "structural coupling," where two systems accommodate one another to create a new set of relationships.

"All of this experience with animals has helped me to learn to read nonverbal signals. Herding cattle is an interesting game. It's a very powerful learning experience for learning both to be in harmony with the situation and to exercise some authority over the action."

Early Introduction to Different Cultures and Passion for Ancient, Exotic Lands

"Another element of my childhood was working with the Mexican ranch hands who didn't speak English. I used to go down and visit the families in their compound on the ranch, and I early on had a fascination and appreciation for other cultures.

"So there I was riding horses, helping to organize the sheep shearing, hanging out with the Mexicans, and, at the same time, also collecting stamps and reading books about long ago and faraway places like Egypt and Africa. I was really interested in ancient cultures and wanted to be an archaeologist."

The groundwork was being laid for Barlow's later social work activities and her personal quest to see foreign lands firsthand. But deeper levels of understanding were woven into her earliest experiences through a complicated and troubling family situation.

"I now realize that part of me was escaping into both the ranch work and the obsession with the ancient past to avoid dealing with my family dynamics. I had the feeling that I had been born in the middle of the movie. My parents and my brother all had their own tragic scenarios in place by the time I was born. I had the feeling that the movie wasn't about me and that I had to figure out the plot. My father had a heart attack when I was two and spent the next nine years dying. It was like a long, melodramatic opera. Again, this situation fostered that deep need in me to decipher subtle messages and patterns.

Further Development of Flexibility in Working with Diverse Peoples

"After I got out of college, I decided I wanted to be a social worker. In Austin, Texas, the home of the University of Texas, everybody wanted to be a social worker. I was the first person to ever score one hundred on the social worker test, so I got a job. Part of that job was to visit old people in ten rural counties around Austin. It was the most joyous job I ever had. I would drive out into the countryside to old farmhouses and shantytowns. Each little home was like an entire universe unto itself. You never knew who was going to open the door that day. People would tell me their entire lives. I remember one woman who was over a hundred years old and a former slave."

It was not long before the confluence of her passion for foreign cultures and her desire to help others came together in yet another outreach position working on a joint assignment for the federal Office of Child Development and the American Academy of Pediatrics. The territory for this job included Guam, Saipan, the Trust Territories of the Pacific, Hawaii, California, and Nevada. "I found myself visiting families in migrant camps, Indian reservations, and atolls where people wore only loincloths and tattoos," she recalled. "It was an incredibly awakening experience."

Traveling the World to Meet the Self: Using Intuitive Guidance

By the age of thirty, Barlow had earned a degree in visual anthropology and photography despite her heavy work and travel schedule. "I finally took a year off work and went around the world. I was exhilarated going to all these exotic locations like Cairo, the Sahara, Kathmandu, and the Himalayas, but halfway around the world, it suddenly hit me that I was now heading back home. I had no idea what I wanted to do. One afternoon I was sitting on a clear, pink rock ledge overlooking the Mediterranean, headed to Turkey and Afghanistan. I did a visualization meditation to ask where to live and what to do with my life. I got an image of a farmhouse completely surrounded by rolling hills. I had another image of a blackboard with hundreds of symbols on it."

On returning home, Barlow began to search for the farmhouse she had seen in her meditation. Her quest led her to Northern California. "I discovered that Sonoma County matched my vision, but after weeks of searching, I finally gave up. After a week later, I found an ad in a local newspaper that said, Old House, Large Yard. When I drove down the road to see the house, I immediately recognized it as the house in my visualization. It was a two-hundred-acre ranch, complete with cows."

DEEPENING OF PASSIONS THROUGH DEPTH PSYCHOLOGY AND SPIRITUAL PRACTICE

"That blackboard I saw in the meditation turned into a master's program in archetypal psychology at Sonoma State University. Another class I took, called Seminar in Zazen, turned into a twenty-five-year Zen practice with Kwong Roshi." [Note: See interview with Kwong Roshi in *The Purpose of Your Life*.]

Those two interests led her, at age forty, to another trip, this time a five-year pilgrimage to India, documenting the worship of Shiva in his myriad names and forms. This trip culminated in a trip to Mt. Kailas in Tibet—and again the question of what to do on her return to the States.

"I remember now that the answer that came in my meditation was *Thy will be done.* So I placed myself in the service of something that could not be named, but it was in the language of the Thou and Thy, that is to say, not the profane but the sacred.

"So many of these life experiences were about being able to stand with multiple perspectives. I had to withhold rational judgment and to be able to hold more than one set of cultural assumptions, and move freely between these different zones I've mentioned. Moving through different cultures and being present in a defocused, open way to catch the patterns is just like catching the horse before the sun is up. This is a good way to be a wanderer in the world, particularly if you are a photographer, and I think it's a good way in general to live your life. You learn to be in synch with a moving situation, which is not jarring to others. You learn to synchronize your movements and posture in order to simply observe."

ALLOWING SYNCHRONICITY TO MOVE HER INTO
THE RIGHT PLACE AT THE RIGHT TIME

Synchronicities continued to play a huge part in moving Barlow ever forward to develop her life purpose. A job as the photo editor of a book in the HarperCollins *Day in the Life* series fell through at the last minute, and she was forced to entertain a possibility she would not otherwise have considered.

"I looked in the newspaper and saw a position as executive director of a think tank founded by Fritjof Capra. I got the job, and since that time we have transformed into a foundation that fosters children's experience and understanding of the natural world. Our work at the foundation is at the confluence of three streams of understanding: The first is the theory of living systems articulated by Fritjof Capra, Joanna Macy, and others; secondly, Native American wisdom, taught primarily by Jeannette Armstrong, an Okanagan wisdom keeper; and thirdly, systemic school reform working with local teachers and state educators.

"For the last eight years, I've been working with many incredible teachers of all kinds—public school teachers, authors, visionaries—all of whom are obviously living their life purposes. For example, I believe that Fritjof Capra and his pioneering theories of living systems; Joanna Macy and her work as a Buddhist scholar, systems theorist, and antinuclear activist; and Jeannette Armstrong, with her centuries-old tradition of living in harmony with the earth are together bringing to us the urgency and gravity of our need to experience and understand the natural world and be at home in it. They are reminding us of our affinity within the web of life and to one another. I genuinely believe their work, and the work of many others among us, is to be the conscience of humanity. It makes decipherable the message I received in Tibet, *Thy will be done.*

After a moment's reflection, Barlow looked at me and said, "In India when you have a confluence of three streams, it's called a *sangam*, which is considered an extraordinarily auspicious place in which one can glimpse the sacred. Where these three come together, there is a fourth, mythical, river implied, which runs beneath. Since we are working on these three streams, we know there is a fourth stream, which is the sacred. This gives great meaning to my work."

EXERCISES

✔ Begin your own collection of stories of people whose outstanding service you admire. The more you surround yourself with inspiring role models of courage and pioneering innovation, the more you will attract those people into your life—and the more you will attract opportunities for your own contribution.

✔ What area of service most attracts you? Jot down a note on page 238 of your profile sheet.

PART SIX

MOVING FORWARD
INTO THE
TWENTY-FIRST CENTURY

CHAPTER 15

Being on Purpose in the New Millennium

One of the most puzzling aspects of evolution is the evidence from the fossil record that the progress of evolution has not been a monotonous progression from simple to more complex organisms, through random mutation and natural selection. Rather, there are long periods during which relatively few new forms appear, and a few much narrower periods . . . during which there is a veritable explosion of new forms, many of which seem to have suddenly sprung into existence as though Nature were saying, "Let's try out this new organism and see how it fares."

—WILLIS HARMAN[1]

How old will you be on December 31, 1999? What issues do you think will be important to you then? How many years of experience will you bring to that moment? What dreams do you bring to the threshold? What fears? What vision of the future do you see for yourself and your friends, your family members, your community, your country, your planet?

All of us will be together in that second of transition, when we leave behind certain ways of life and continue the movement into possibilities, fluctuating global chaos, synchronistic solutions, and hard decisions. What do we have in common? What do we bring to the global table at the local level? How do we make our life count? In the great acceleration that is taking place, the new millennium is sure to bring us as many questions as answers. There is no way to know what will turn out to be the most important tiny shifts, the most transforming seeds, or the most troublesome flaws in our thinking, feeling, and doing. Anything is possible.

WHAT DO WE KNOW?

For all the technological choreography we depend on for survival in the so-called developed countries, the fact remains we are still humans who must eat, drink, eliminate, relate, procreate, and ponder our heavenly position in the cosmos. Millions of us experience the imbalances of a life lived for the most part disconnected from the energizing and healing influence of the natural world. Millions of us experience daily deprivations of food, pure air and water, shelter, fulfilling livelihood, time, and other resources. Millions of us experience war, torture, pain, and suffering of every kind. And yet the human spirit reaches beyond what can be endured and puts down roots between the stones. Every day the hero and heroine in us struggle to move toward the light. What we know is that to live the life we were born to live is a great gift, but it demands that we wake up to who we really are. This is the purpose of life. To be human is to become conscious of ourselves deep down in our frailties and failures, deep inside our confusion of hopes and fears—to the genius of our multidimensional nature. The purpose of life is to wake up to the gift of the *experience* of life.

ANGELA AND THE YEAR 2000

Someone once told me that there are two ways to avoid being on purpose. One is to let others define us. The second is to be afraid to take the first step.

One sunny morning I was having tea and toast with my friend Angela, whom I also interviewed for *The Purpose of Your Life*. As readers may remember, she was the Idaho beauty queen who had two disastrous marriages, whose fiancé died jogging on the eve of their wedding, and whose eldest daughter became severely brain-damaged following a fall from a horse. I asked Angela, now sixty-four, how she saw her life going forward into the new millennium. After a few moments of reflection, she quietly said, "I see an image of an open lotus flower with each petal representing one of my life experiences. The flower is radiating energy from all the pain that I have endured. For years I've had the deep-seated fear that I was always just about to be trapped by the temptations of my ego desires. For example, I wanted to marry a rich man. I went looking for them, so that I could have the trappings of security and success. I always felt just on the edge of making a fatal decision that would bury my soul. My self-talk was telling me that I was stupid, that I was an impostor, that I had no credibility in comparison to others. But I know now that my integrity, faith, and good intention went deeper than I had thought. The truth is that I look at my life now and feel very good—and I'm still here, which surprises me given my family history of cancer and all the problems I've faced. I am very proud of who I am and no longer make those disparaging comparisons about credibility. I'm still pretty good-looking and healthy for my age. I have extraordinary friends. Money in the bank. I'm handling my daughter's situation as best I can. I love my garden and my chosen work creating peace and harmony and healing environments.

"I have had such grief, and yet I am still able to look at the beauty of what I have been forced to learn. From here on out I want to completely respect myself and not ever again doubt that I do have integrity and good intention, because I know how to stay in my right mind and right heart. My purpose for 2000 and beyond is to respect the illumination that is in this opened flower and to reflect that light."

YOUR OWN SYMBOL

What symbol best represents you or your life? Close your eyes and let go of your stream of thoughts. Allow a strong, persistent symbol, sound, message, or color to arise in your mind. Record any insights here. ____

_____

_____

_____

THE UPSIDE OF GLOBAL TRANSITION

Tom Atlee, coeditor of a small book called *Awakening: The Upside of Y2K*, has been fully engaged in researching collaborative techniques for several years. Founder of The Co-Intelligence Institute, he is now actively involved in community preparedness and education about the ramifications of problems stemming from computer breakdowns during the date change on January 1, 2000.

After reading his book, I called Tom to find out how his awareness of technological and ecological global problems was affecting his own life purpose. Tom has been a longtime advocate for sustainable technology, renewable forms of energy, and community cohesiveness. He believes that the beneficial side of the computer problem will accelerate and initiate much-needed ecological and social changes that ultimately will bring more harmony and community resilience. Rather than isolating this phenomenon as merely a technological blunder, Tom sees it as forcing people to recognize the need for cooperative action. His advice? "Get to know your neighbors."

The big question is: says Atlee, "Do we know how to live *together* in one place if resources like food, water, fuel, and electricity suddenly disappear?" Can we think cooperatively and bioregionally?

"In the new society, we will have to realize that no one of us can decide what is the truth. Where each of us puts our attention does matter; however, it doesn't determine what happens. I can be a major factor, but I can't decide what happens. Part of my previous work prepared me to understand, for example, that our national and regional diversity is a powerful resource, instead of a problem. It taught me that it's possible to evoke the natural power of systems to self-organize and heal themselves, rather than *force* them into particular solutions. Like in aikido, our greatest strength is in moving with the energy that's already there.

"There's a concept I like very much that outlines the power of the self-organizing principle. Harrison Owen surveyed people at the Open Space Conference, and he found that what people liked the most about the conference were the coffee breaks. He began to rethink what a conference is and began to use what people were interested in to create the conference. A conference should be a place where everyone who comes is passionate about what is being discussed. If not, why come? In an Open Space Conference, there are four principles: (1) It starts when it starts, (2) whoever comes are the right people, (3) whatever happens is the only thing that could happen, and (4) when it's over, it's over. The other key thing is the law of two feet. When you find yourself not learning or contributing, it's time to go somewhere else. This is great advice for living in the next millennium.

"When I'm blocked, I ask myself, 'How can I change my consciousness enough so that I am learning and contributing right here?' Our society is not set up for us to find our life purpose. Everything is set up for us not to know that. Society, schools, institutions, corporations are always trying to channel us into what is needed by someone else.

"Going into the millennium, we have to work now with all levels of reality simultaneously—individual, group, national, global. We need to handle all the social, psychological, physical, and relational fields of life. The question is, 'How can we be more intelligent together than by ourselves?' People look blank when I talk about co-intelligence, but they laugh when I say it's the opposite of co-stupidity.

"I think we need new storytellers. We can't tell the same old myth of the Lone Ranger anymore—the lone hero. And it needs to be done soon.

"There has never been an opportunity like this in my lifetime. That's what gets me up in the morning. My current purpose right now includes training myself to keep returning to the possibilities, like returning to the breath when I meditate."

"I believe we have to be super-proactive now, but that is terrifying to most people. The answer is to work together, because nobody can do this alone. We are going to be forced to make these choices sooner or later. If life is an adventure of discovering who we are, then the year 2000 is when we find out." (Tom's website address is www.co-intelligence.org.)

HEALING AND EDUCATING

Rick Ingrasci has traditional credentials as a medical doctor with a master's degree in public health—having trained at Cornell University Medical College and Harvard—as well as the right instincts to follow a life purpose centered on education and healing. The evolution of these interests finds him in 1999 still bent on healing, but on a global scale possible only through a network of relationships with other visionaries and the use of the Internet. "I never practiced traditional medicine. Early on, I recognized my values and needs marched to a different drummer. I learned a lot about the patterns of disease in medicine, but my interest gravitated to holistic thinkers such as Buckminster Fuller and Marshall McLuhan. What shocked me was that so few physicians actually looked at people holistically.

"I got involved with the consciousness movement in the sixties, the antiwar movement, and the exploration of spirituality, meditation, and yoga. I also studied humanistic psychology and group dynamics. I began to associate with radical software video artists and explored the then-current technology for consciousness expansion. By the time I got to public health, I had a clear picture of how communications media could be used for public health and preventive medicine.

"Since most diseases of civilization are chronic degenerative diseases associated with mind-set and lifestyle, it seemed it should be possible to develop educational processes that deal with self-healing, using biofeedback and inner-directed disciplines. These were tools that could be used and shared through mass media. I had a sense even then that there would be some form of what we now call the Internet."

For several years, Ingrasci focused on alternative health methods and holistic education, founding Interface, a holistic center in Boston, as well as a series of group practices that involved a variety of disciplines and techniques that have since become part of our mainstream culture. Cofounder of the American Holistic Medical Association and the Physicians for Social Responsibility (physicians concerned about nuclear proliferation) and coauthor of the book *Chop Wood Carry Water: A Guide to Finding Spirituality in Everyday Life,* Ingrasci was also the health editor for *New Age Journal.* In 1991 he and his wife, Peggy Taylor, moved to Whidbey Island, Washington, and founded the Whidbey Institute, a learning center with an ecospiritual focus, as well as a business called The CyberCafe and Bookstore, an arm of the institute.

"I've always had a keen interest in using the media for cultural healing, and that early interest is what I have returned to in the nineties. The insights about my life's work in the sixties have come into deeper focus in the nineties. With the development of the World Wide Web, I decided to get involved in new media. The CyberCafe has a fast connection to the Internet, which allows us to do social experiments with virtual community development.

"The focus of my work has become community development both locally and globally. I do invitational conferences that focus on the spirit of community and how one fosters that. This ties in with virtual community development, as local communities can connect with each other through the Internet.

"The best thinking on the Y2K problem acknowledges that while what we are facing is a complex technical systems failure, the real issue is a social problem. What we are really faced with is the challenge of how we are living our lives. We have become dependent on a global computer and energy grid that is not interruptible. Y2K is what's called a 'teachable moment.' It's a time in history that people, out of concern for survival issues, will be looking at the question, 'How do we want to live?' We are not living in a sustainable way right now.

"My focus is on educating communities about how to become resilient, which means being capable of adapting and responding to whatever changes happen in the environment, just like the conscious-ness movement has been saying for forty years."

What is Ingrasci's advice for those of us searching for life purpose at the time of the new millennium?

"Recognize that every crisis is an opportunity to reframe how you choose to live. We've created almost a religious blind faith about sci-ence and technology, forgetting to ask the deeper questions of mean-ing and value. I don't think it's an accident that at the very moment when we move into the first second of the new millennium, we are forced to address how we want to live."

What practical advice does he have for those of us who feel our pur-pose is to help through the transition?

"Educate yourself on what's out there. Read books like John McNight's *Building Community from the Inside Out*. Get involved with your neighbors. Recognize that in any crisis, the solutions will emerge by simply coming together as a community. If you are alone and overwhelmed, you tend to go into survivalism, thinking, 'I have to do it all myself.' If you're with your friends and family and neighbor-hood, all kinds of creative possibilities start to emerge. The key is to be open-minded and educate yourself, and then to act in concert with neighbors locally. You don't have to solve the problem for the planet. Take care of those in your community and be willing to share yourself with others. The key is preparation."

THE DEAL OF THE MILLENNIUM

Bobbie McMorrow is an insider in the elite, powerful world of mergers and acquisitions. Usually the only woman at the table, she sits with the men who make business decisions that have mind-boggling ramifica-tions for the future. "I call myself a synthesizing visionary," says

McMorrow, who has her own business providing executive search, career counseling, and business management. "I love the quote by poet William Stafford, 'It's the job of the artist to get up ahead of the world, and try to define what it's attempting to be.' This is a theme for the end of the millennium. We're trying to create new models for ourselves. Even with all the developments in humanistic psychology, spirituality, human rights, feminism, global awareness, and environmental movements, there is still a lot of mass confusion about what life is supposed to be. We're still stuck between different structures."

McMorrow knows what she's talking about when it comes to strategy and vision for the new millennium. International businesses are largely run by lawyers, she notes, and with the huge acceleration of British and American law firms opening up offices around the world, there is a big demand for lawyers. Her job is to find those lawyers and other high-level executives who will become the forces behind international business.

"I do *their* deals," says McMorrow. "It's interesting, but by and large, most of these lawyers are limited by their own thinking. They work tremendously long hours and are too busy to stop and look at their own lives. And their perspective is limited by their training. They're trained to think about building barriers, not to come up with totally new models.

"In seventeen years I have never sat at the table with another woman—unless she is the candidate for hire—when a firm is committing tens of millions of dollars. This has put me in a unique position to see how men see the world, their grasp of business and what's important."

From Teacher to Executive Recruiter

McMorrow was plunged into the world of high finance within the space of eighteen months after being a preschool and elementary school teacher for thirteen years. She started her own schools for learning-disabled children and worked with terminally ill children. Working in the barrio on a federal project, earning about seven thousand dollars a year, she was unable to pay for a special school for her son, who had severe learning disabilities. She began to research the job market in an attempt to increase her income. She opted for a commission-based business but didn't want to sell products. "Selling products seemed boring. I liked people, so I thought, well, I could sell people, so I went into executive search. I had to start my own business because I couldn't find a job!"

Isolation Is a Danger

"How might these volatile times affect our own life purpose?" I asked Ms. McMorrow. "What should we be looking at? How can we best weather these difficult times?"

"One of the biggest problems in our culture is isolation," she replied. "If we continue to separate ourselves from each other, we will never get out of the confusion. The answers we need are already present on the planet, but because we are isolated and separated from one another, we can't see the answers. We're going to have to be able to communicate what's really going on everywhere, tell the truth even when it's not popular, and trust that our perceptions are necessary to the whole."

Past Challenges Give Us a Unique Authority and Power

"Personally, I have gone through just about all the challenges a woman can go through in life and business. In the future, we are going to have to be able to think on our feet even more. What we did yesterday may not be relevant today or in a year from now. The best thing I have found is to establish in myself the authority of my own life. For example, no one is just like you. You have lived through things that have given you wisdom. Acknowledge that. Draw from that place of strength no matter what you are doing.

"Many of us are simply not aware of the great power our unique life experiences have given us. Most of us have had difficult or devastating challenges, which we have overcome. There is an inherent energy in those experiences, much like a power chip. Our life purpose gives us those situations we need to wake us up. Many people forget that Gandhi was a lawyer but he could hardly feed his family. He wasn't a very good lawyer. He had been on his way down to South Africa to help another Indian with a business contract when he got thrown off the train for being an Indian, even though he was of the Brahman class. That experience impelled him to wake up to racial and class injustice. He became impassioned about human rights, and his mission was activated.

We Empower Ourselves from the Inside Out

"I do believe that there is an energy in the world that does try to keep us in our place. Status quo institutions don't want everyone to become empowered. They aren't going to hand us the keys to the kingdom. We have to find our power first in ourselves. We do that by rethinking our pivotal experiences—the ones we judged to be so negative—and finding the specific perspective or strength we gained from having gone through them. I've been through a good deal of family abuse and dysfunction, but every one of those times gave me a source of energy to draw from. *All* of our experience supports our inborn purpose.

"In my work I talk with very successful professional people who come from extremely elite educational backgrounds and all kinds of achievements. Many of them are highly successful Afro-American, Asian, and Hispanic executive men and women, all of whom are making between $300,000 and $700,000 a year. Yet they are all trying to figure out how they're getting blocked in the world! Almost none of them are blaming the white culture, because they have all had great success. But I hear them say, 'I just don't see how I can break into the big time.' "

We Can Use the Strength Gained from Pivotal Experiences

"I see two things working. First, there's always some reality to racial prejudice. Second, I can see that the minority-group executives looked to the already successful white role models for the rules of how to achieve success. They were smart, and saw, okay you have to go to Harvard, get an MBA, become a lawyer, marry the right person, and so on. They followed what others were doing, with no thought as to what their own unique life purpose might be. I see them fighting their own cultures, trying to stand out or stand away from their heritage. They aren't using the strength and power of the black, Asian, and Hispanic cultures. They are trying to be white. I believe they have to go back to the power of the roots of their own life path in order to find the fulfillment they want. This is exactly what I had to do when I was changing from being a teacher to working in the echelons of Wall Street.

"In a year and a half, I went from teaching preschool to being involved in the biggest deals on Wall Street in mergers and acquisitions. I was sitting at these conference tables, and I didn't even have a business background. I didn't have an MBA. It was very intimidating to sit there with these powerful men with Ph.D.s and years and years of experience in high finance. Sure, I had developed a good 'rap,' but it was just marketing stuff. I didn't really know what was going on in the financial market. How was I going to handle that?

"In order to do the work before me, I had to find a source of strength and confidence in myself. What I realized was that I, too, had a wealth of human experience, but not in the field of finance. I remember in the beginning going into these meetings, and I would find myself at One Wall Street with five or six New York power brokers. I had to think fast.

"The first thing I had to do was be able to get out of my own fear. I needed to be able to sit at that table and hold my own position. They, on their side, needed to feel that they could trust *me*. Most of us believe that people evaluate us on the basis of our education, our resume, our reputation, our successes—which, of course, is true to some extent. However, the real trust comes when you see that some-one is speaking from his or her own authority. This is not bludgeoning authority. It's meeting people with a level of awareness and intelli-gence that rings true, and this could very well be street intelligence. That is what makes you trustworthy. You also have to have a level of enthusiasm for who the other person is and really listen to them with attention. People like that. By the way, these are all of the things a woman develops just by being a woman in the world!"

Power Comes from Being in Touch with the Authority of Your Own Life Experiences

"So in the beginning I knew I had no authority in the financial world, but I literally heard a voice in my head that said, 'You have sat with dying children.' This is how I knew the universe was helping me. Immediately, it clicked in my mind, 'Power comes from being in touch with the authority of your own life and what you have learned.' We don't really acknowledge who we are and what we have been through. We diminish ourselves. We always believe that who we are comes from somewhere else."

Does she recommend having a five-year plan for the new millen-nium?

Five-Year Plans Work Only If You Are in Integrity and the Plans Are Flexible

"I've never thought ahead to what would happen in five or ten years. I've always just done what was fun at that time. I think five-year plans are more meaningless now than ever before, unless you have a way to keep your plan entirely open and flexible! If your plan is based on integrity and not on goals, your plan will help you stay focused. Integrity is knowing who you are and what you value and going for that. There are law firms whose goal is to make extraordinary amounts of money. By staying in the integrity of their goal to make money, their five-and ten-year plans will probably work. You might not agree with their integrity, but they know who they are, and they don't get off their plan to make money. They don't suddenly decide next year to become a nonprofit orphanage. I think integrity means sticking to the purpose of who you say you are. Usually five-year plans don't work because people have not defined what it is that is their integrity."

Going Back to What Really Matters in Life

"Women have to remember their integrity of being a woman and not fall into the trap of trying to convert to being a man. The advantage of being a woman is that we can hold onto the integrity of what it means to birth a child, dig in a garden, cook a meal, and give and receive support from our friends. I'm glad I got started late in the business world at age thirty-seven, because I'd already tapped into what had meaning to me. Once you have a sense of what you're about, then you can have a five-year plan, but you still have to be open and flexible!"

The Blindness of Running as Fast as We Can Without Vision

"Nobody can figure out what's going on anymore. This latest financial crisis has thrown even financial experts into a tailspin. Even though they're making money on it, they're living on adrenaline. They're tapping their fingers all the time, talking a mile a minute. They're not getting along with their wives. They're racing all over the world. They don't know if they're making the right decisions.

"Until we stop our obsession with making business be entirely about raising stock share prices, we won't be able to find a new way. The economy isn't based on real goods and services anymore. Most of the energy is spent on empty deals, endlessly divesting, merging, divesting, merging. The business vocabulary of the 'bottom line' and 'doing the deal' has completely invaded the mentality of politics and almost everything else. This is scary.

"On a personal level, this type of business thinking gets people off their life purposes at an early age. People believe what business and politics are selling them. The young people I work with all bought into this myth that they had to go to Harvard and get their MBA. Now they're in these positions they lusted after all their life, and they find them to be hollow. The smart ones are going all the way back—going to therapy, taking care of their physical health, and looking for a new perspective, looking at real values. They are realizing that what they thought was the purpose of their life doesn't hold any value for them and that they are going to have to create something new."

Life Experiences Are Clues to Life Purpose

"I believe that our lives give us the clues of what that purpose is. In working with children, I've often seen how we get them off their purpose almost immediately. I remember one mother who was going to take her child out of public school and put him in private school because he was almost six years old and couldn't read. All his ancestors had gone to Harvard. I said, 'Maybe he's supposed to be a famous artist.' She couldn't hear it. She was taking her child's life and defining it by a rigorous set of values that had nothing to do with who he was.

"On the other end of the spectrum, I have met dozens of older executives who are burned out and trying to edge out of the rat race. They're already making at least a million a year, and they want to know what else they could do. I've said many times, 'Maybe the question isn't *What is the next position?* but *Who do you want to become as a person?* They look at me as if I am crazy. My words have zero effect. But I think that's the question we need to ask in our fifties. Who is it we want to become?"

What Are You Going to Contribute When the Universe Calls Your Name?

McMorrow likes to quote a favorite teacher, Dr. Morris Netherton, the father of regression therapy, who said, "There comes a time in everyone's life when the universe calls your name." Suddenly there is a clarion call. We know the world is going to be thrown into great changes. What are we going to contribute? The world needs new prototypes for the actualized human being.

"I believe we can start by understanding our own inner masculine and feminine natures and not misjudge them or destroy their essential powers, which were designed by the universe. You have to be able to recognize that part of yourself which wants to do something bold, creative, and new—the masculine—and that part of yourself that demands divine, soulful work and relationships—the feminine. You honor yourself and all of life by being a person of integrity."

Going Forward with Balance and Integrity

"A purpose statement for the millennium has to come from that place of balanced and respected energy. Our actions have to come from that foundation. It's like tai chi. If you don't gather energy properly, you can't go forward. You'll be out of balance. It's so clear that you have to drop back and gather, and then move forward. If you try only to move forward, you'll exhaust yourself. We're exhausting the patriarchy. We won't have to bring it down. It's exhausting itself. I have been astounded at the level of grief I have seen in the faces of so many older men and women. They don't realize the kind of power they have to create whole universes. Is that a big enough purpose?

Our Life Purpose in the Future Depends on Being Deep into Our Humanity

"Our first life purpose is to be deep into our experience of what it means to be human. So often achievement takes us out of our humanity. If we are out of our humanity, then we are not really living our purpose. When we are in our humanity, that's when we are powerful. In the new millennium, we need to be able to find our internal truth and sit at the table in our humanity.

Personal Review of Bobbie McMorrow's Story

✔ *What stood out for you in the preceding story?* Answer any of the following questions that speak to you. Jot down any insights you gain on page 239 of your profile sheet.
✔ *What past challenges have given you a unique authority and power?* Bobbie McMorrow had deep experiences with family dysfunction, as a mother with a learning-disabled son, as a teacher in the barrio,

and as a therapist with terminally ill children. She had experience helping overcome hurdles. What area of authority have your experiences provided *you*? Write them here. Draw upon that wisdom next time you are feeling fearful or overwhelmed. _____

_____

_____

_____

✔ *Isolation is a danger*: Write about any isolation in your own life. How might you balance your isolation/focus/production time with quality relationship time? _____

_____

_____

_____

✔ *Empower yourself from the inside out*. What do you really know about? Name at least five things you are an expert in. Jot these down on page 239 of your profile sheet. _____

   1. _____
   2. _____
   3. _____
   4. _____
   5. _____

✔ *Use the strength gained from pivotal experiences*. Write down three pivotal experiences (even if you have written about these in other chapters of this book) and what they have taught you.

   1. _____ taught me _____

   _____

   2. _____ taught me _____

   _____

   3. _____ taught me _____

✔ *Power comes from being in touch with the authority of your own life*. Close your eyes and imagine yourself at work or in any situation where you feel overwhelmed, helpless, one down, or resentful. Imagine yourself coming into the power of who you are. What does this feel like? Look like? Sound like? Taste like? Write down your impressions here. _____

_____

_____

✔ *Practice filling yourself with the deep, soulful essence of who you are before going out of the house for the day. How does your experience differ from before?* _____

_____

_____

✔ *Five-year plans work only if you are in integrity.* If you were to write a statement of what you want your life to be like—in its general feeling tone—what would that be? Make a sketchy five-year plan here. How open and flexible does it seem to be? What is the core value that you must have? _____

_____

_____

_____

_____

✔ Transfer the core points in your description of your life plan to page 239 of your profile sheet.

✔ *What really matters in life.* If you had only six months to live, what would you do? Transfer your answer to your profile sheet, page 239.

_____

_____

_____

✔ *The blindness of running as fast as we can without vision.* When was the last time you sat down and reviewed where you are in life? When was the last time you had a real conversation about shared values with your spouse or partner? Is it time for that now? Take a moment to look at your calendar. Can you make time to reserve a date with yourself? _____

_____

_____

✔ *What are you going to contribute when the universe calls your name?*

_____

_____

_____

✔ *Life purpose depends on being deep into our humanity.* Write a few words about how deep you are into your own humanity, how connected you feel to your species and other species, and how you feel about the care of your planetary home. _____

_____

_____

_____

_____

✔ *Me and the new millennium.* Review all your responses to the preceding questions. Circle the *most highly charged words* from your writing, and transfer those words to the space below. _____

_____

_____

I AM IN INTEGRITY
COMPLETE THE SENTENCES IN THE CIRCLE TO
CHARACTERIZE THE INTEGRITY YOU WISH TO TAKE INTO
THE NEW MILLENIUM.

I am a person who
_____

_____

_____

_____

I wish to add to _____   I feel a deep authority about

_____   _____

_____   _____

_____   _____

_____   _____

I am willing to _____   _____ I support

_____   _____

_____   _____

_____   _____

_____   _____

_____ I look forward to being _____

_____

_____

_____

I don't believe it was an accident that the insights of *The Celestine Prophecy* came along five years ago, just as we were beginning the countdown for the millennium shift. Those of us who care about people, who care about the Earth, are now being called forth in every walk of life to make a difference for the future of our planet. The year 2000 is the convergence point for the multidimensional streams of interconnected global technology, deep spirituality, economic volatility, and major cultural transitions, spiced with imminent earth changes. Will it be a catalyst for a more healthy, satisfying, and just life for all? Can we hold a positive vision for a future of greater cooperation and widespread abundance?

Remember that you were born with a purpose and that you chose to be born in this time frame to help hold the vision for the future. Trust your instincts and intuitive guidance. Know that when you are thinking about someone, you are in telepathic communication at that moment. Learn what helps you stay centered, and do more of that. Face each day and what it brings. Let go of trying to control the uncontrollable, and find something positive to add today.

I will remember
To focus on what I want, not what I don't want.
To breathe and remain as calm and centered as possible.
To find strength within myself and trust in the divine power of love.
That there are forces beyond my control, and
My job is to add something positive to each moment.
I am a ray of light and a fountain of good humor,
Allowing my own special life purpose to be used for the common good.

Profile of Purpose

Name _____ Date _____

This section, called the Profile of Purpose, is the place where you can jot down all the insights you have gained and notes you have written to yourself while going through the workbook. It is designed to be a summary of all the ideas you have as you discover and refine your inborn life purpose. As mentioned earlier, the workbook is designed either to be worked in from beginning to end in a linear fashion or to be dipped into at random. Either way, the Profile of Purpose, also called profile sheet, keeps your work in one place, where you can refer to it easily.

Once you have filled in most of this summary, distill the most relevant information and fill in the Master Profile of Purpose that follows these pages. You will then have created your own statement of life purpose. Congratulations!

CHAPTER 1: GETTING STARTED

WHAT I AM LOOKING FOR

Question 1.   What is so important to you that you bought this book to work on finding your life purpose?

_____

_____

Question 2.   What are you looking for?

_____

_____

Question 4.   What would make you happy?

_____

_____

Question 6.   How do you want to feel?

_____

_____

Question 11. If you had the thing that would make a difference in the quality of your life, what would that give you?

_____

_____

Question 13. What would it take for you to be living in total integrity?

_____

_____

Summary of What I Am Looking For

Review your answers. What three words are most highly charged in your profile of what you are looking for?

1. _____

2. _____

3. _____

Insight

The words I selected suggest that what I most need and want is _____

_____

_____

If I had what I wanted right now, I would feel _____

_____

_____

It might smell like, look like, and sound like _____

_____

Insight from Sunni's Story

_____

_____

_____

CHAPTER 2: INITIATION

Notes from your own special day of initiation: _____

_____

_____

_____

_____

_____

My initiation poem: _____

_____

_____

_____

The significance of my personal day of initiation based on numerology:

_____

_____

_____

_____

CHAPTER 3: THE BOTTOM LINES OF MY LIFE PURPOSE—
WHAT FEELS MOST IMPORTANT TO ME

Fill in your answers from the section Drawing
My Current Life Matrix (pages 23–24)

1. *What I love about my life right now* _____

_____

_____

_____

2. *What I want to attract* _____

_____

_____

_____

3. *What I want to release* _____

_____

_____

_____

My top three needs are:
  1. _____
  2. _____
  3. _____

My top need is _____

_____

Insights from my five-minute writing exercise on page 28: _____

_____

_____

_____

According to my most natural and dominant tendency I seem to be a (thinker, mover, feeler, or intuitive)

_____

I can summarize what's my line by saying (from page 30)

_____

_____

My fantasy résumé would look like this:
  The name of the position I am looking for is _____

  _____

  What I want to do in the world is _____

  _____

  My salary is _____

  _____

  My special needs are _____

_____

_____

My qualifications are _____

_____

_____

My special interests are _____

_____

My greatest job and life references are _____

_____

_____

My career niche (page 31) seems to be in the area of _____

_____

How can I allow more of my true nature to shine forth? (from page 34)

_____

_____

_____

What I love to do _____

_____

_____

_____

Insight from David Ish's story: _____

_____

_____

_____

CHAPTER 4: MY LIFE STORY AND WHAT IT TELLS ABOUT ME

Synopsis of how I combine my parental lineages from both sides. Part of my purpose in life is to integrate my mother's and father's natures and perspectives and take these to another level, which means that _____

_____

_____

_____

_____

Synopsis of my family's beliefs about money (from page 44): _____

_____

_____

_____

Synopsis of my beliefs about education and achievement (from page 45):_____

_____

_____

Synopsis of my beliefs about work: _____

_____

_____

_____

The best thing I ever heard someone say about me (from page 47):___

_____

_____

Synopsis of insights about my unconscious ceilings (from page 47): ___

_____

_____

_____

The fairy story suggested by my time line events (from page 60): _____

_____

_____

_____

_____

How I describe myself without referring to what I do for a living (from page 60): _____

_____

_____

_____

_____

My obituary (from page 61): _____

_____

_____

_____

_____

_____

_____

_____

_____

_____

_____

_____

_____

_____

_____

_____

CHAPTER 5: GETTING PAST RESISTANCES

What catches my attention. Synopsize your monthly record of interests as suggested on page 65 (from pages 132–133 in Chapter 9, Tracking Relevant Information). _____

_____

_____

_____

High points of my personal and professional life. From page 65, jot down the highlights of your life that seem to have sprung from your deep-seated purpose, mission, or passion. _____

_____

_____

_____

Thumbnail sketch of someone I admire. By drawing a quick portrait of someone (e.g., a celebrity, your child, or your next-door neighbor), you will be able to notice aspects of yourself that you either use fully now or may develop simply by paying more attention to those qualities in yourself.

The qualities I most admire in _____ are

_____

_____

_____

Select the qualities you most admire in your role model, and write an affirmation stating that you are now using these qualities or talents every day.

I am now using my talents for _____
_____ *every day!*

I am where I need to be today because

_____

_____

_____

_____

What I most want and need is (write your affirmation about what you want, from page 67): _____

_____

_____

_____

What I love to do is (What three words describe you best? What insight did you receive from your writing exercise on page 75?)
The three words that describe me best are:

(1) _____

(2) _____

(3) _____

My insight is _____

_____

_____

_____

_____

What I am looking for is (from page 75): _____

_____

_____

_____

_____

What I think stops me from having what I am looking for (from page 75): _____

_____

_____

How I can get around the obstacle that I think stops me: _____

_____

_____

_____

All I have to do is what I love to do and am good at, which is _____

_____

_____

Write down several of your favorite ideas that help keep you sane and centered (for use during those "middle-of-the-night" blues):

1. _____

2. _____

3. _____

4. _____

5. _____

Build a support group. List the people you feel closest to. Is there a chance you could call them together for an informal meeting to help you solve a problem or to brainstorm together? If you don't know many people, could you ask those you do know to bring along good friends of theirs? What does your intuition tell you about finding compatible people? _____

_____

_____

_____

_____

CHAPTER 6: TEN COMMONLY ASKED QUESTIONS
ABOUT FINDING RIGHT LIVELIHOOD

Summarize the insights you received from reading any of the ten questions and doing the exercises in Chapter 6. It's not necessary to respond to all the questions. Concentrate on the questions that apply to you and your current situation.

Insights from Question 1. *What if I don't know what my passion is?*
   I feel most at home doing (from page 82)

_____

_____

_____

Activities with which I have lost track of time (from page 83):

_____

_____

_____

What I would do if I knew I could not fail (from page 83):

_____

_____

_____

Insights from Question 2. *How do I transition out of a job where I have a secure paycheck?*
   My present job is out of alignment with my values and what I hold most sacred because (from page 84)

_____

_____

What would make me happiest is

_____

_____

Insights from Question 3. *What if my new business doesn't seem to be getting off the ground?*
   What do I want?

_____

_____

What's stopping me from having this? (Describe your *belief* about the frustration.)

_____

_____

What attitude, behavior, or expectation do I need to change?

_____

The emotional issue in my life that has not been fully resolved is

_____

_____

Insights from Question 4: *How do I define a new career when I don't know what I want?*

Write down any of the suggestions on pages 89–90 that energized you (even a little bit).

1. _____
2. _____
3. _____
4. _____

Insights from Question 5: *If I have talent, how do I make that talent support me?*

Write down any of the suggestions on pages 90–91 that energized you (even a little bit).

_____

_____

_____

Insights from Question 6: *What if I think I'm too old to start over?*

What matters to you? How can you foster that in the world? Jot down any of your insights that energized you (even a little bit).

_____

_____

_____

Insights from Question 7. *What if my partner is skeptical or not encouraging about my goals?*

Write down any of the suggestions on page 93 that energized you (even a little bit).

_____

_____

_____

Insights from Question 8. *Should I go back to school?*
   What's your motivation for going back to school? What does your
   instinct tell you? What kinds of classes would *really* excite you?

_____

_____

_____

Insights from Question 9. *Should I have a plan, or just follow what life
gives me?*
   What works for you? What does your intuition say?

_____

_____

_____

Insights from Question 10. *How can I balance career, marriage, and
family?*
   What does your gut instinct tell you about this?

_____

_____

_____

CHAPTER 7: "BUT WHAT DO I *DO*?"

Describe who you are without talking about your present or past job
titles (from page 109): _____

_____

_____

_____

What is coming into my field of vision or action (from page 109):

_____

_____

_____

What would bring more adventure into my life (from page 110):

_____

_____

_____

What would make the biggest positive difference in my life (from page 111): _____

_____

_____

_____

What insights from Kim's story stood out for me (from page 116):

_____

_____

_____

CHAPTER 8: WRITING A WORKING PURPOSE STATEMENT

My working purpose statement (from page 121) is _____

_____

_____

_____

What touched me most about Linda's story (from page 124) was

_____

_____

_____

CHAPTER 9: TRACKING RELEVANT INFORMATION

The insights about what would make me happy (from page 130) are:

_____

_____

_____

What I notice about the things that interested me this month (from page 133) is: _____

_____

_____

_____

What stood out for me about Louella's story (from page 135) is _____

_____

_____

_____

Question 1. The best contribution I made today was (from page 137) _____

_____

_____

Question 2. I can see that I am already in the flow of my life purpose because (from page 137)

_____

_____

_____

Question 3. What is working great in my life is (from page 137)

_____

_____

_____

_____

The values my feminine thinks are important are (from page 141)

_____

_____

_____

The kind of help my masculine energy has requested is (from page 141) _____

_____

_____

Notes about my Personal Year (from page 144):

_____

_____

CHAPTER 10: FUN STUFF—MAKE YOUR OWN ORACLES

Keep track of the questions and insights you receive from your cards for one month. Describe any pattern you find. _____

_____

_____

_____

_____

_____

_____

_____

_____

CHAPTER 11: DOWNLOADING AND OFFLOADING FEAR, BLOCKS, AND RESISTANCES

Can you remember being criticized for something when you were a child that has turned out to be a valuable characteristic or asset today?

_____

_____

_____

_____

What insights stood out for you in Nancy's story of the void? (from page 162) _____

_____

_____

Record here any notes from your Obstacle Meditation (from pages 163–164). _____

_____

_____

What symbol emerged that represented a creative next step? (from page 165) _____

_____

_____

CHAPTER 12: WHERE WE LOSE POWER

What stood out for me in Bob's story is (from page 169)

_____

_____

_____

What touched me about Mary's story was (from page 180)

_____

_____

_____

CHAPTER 13: CREATING THE MAGIC MAGNETIC CIRCLE

Notes from work done in your support circle: _____

_____

_____

_____

_____

_____

_____

_____

_____

CHAPTER 14: MAKING A DIFFERENCE

What area of service most attracts you? (from page 200) _____

_____

_____

Keep a record here of stories and news articles about inspiring people.

_____

_____

_____

_____

_____

_____

_____

_____

_____

CHAPTER 15: BEING ON PURPOSE IN THE NEW MILLENNIUM

What stood out for me in Bobbie McMorrow's story (from page 216) is

_____

_____

_____

I'm an expert on these five things:

1. _____
2. _____
3. _____
4. _____
5. _____

How do you want to feel in the next few years in the following areas concerning the core points of your life plan?

Physical realm:

_____

_____

Spiritual realm:

_____

_____

Emotional realm:

_____

_____

Mental realm:

_____

_____

Financial realm:

_____

_____

Contribution to the world:

_____

_____

If you had only six months to live, what would you do? (from page 218) _____

_____

_____

What are you going to contribute when the universe calls your name? (from page 218)

_____

_____

_____

My life purpose is

_____

_____

_____

Master Profile of My Life Purpose

"What, then, is the difference," I asked her, "in the way you look at the world now and in the way you looked at it before your experiences?"
"Even though you don't seem different to other people," she replied, "inside your spiritual sense gets stronger. You feel more self-assured that you're on the right track. You're happier, more centered. But it takes a long time until this shows up enough to make you into a different person."

—Harry R. Moody[1]

This section provides a place for you to summarize the wealth of information you have gathered about yourself, what you want, and how you want to feel.

Review all the answers in your Profile of Purpose. First, look for statements you made about your abilities, gifts, and what others say about you. Write the most important characteristics in the section entitled, **What I Have to Offer.**

Next, review the material again regarding the **subjects that have been capturing your attention** since you started working in this workbook. Write those ideas under the section entitled **My Current Interests.**

Write down a piece of wisdom that gives you joy, hope, and energy in the section **My Favorite Inspiring Wisdom.**

What do you think you can say about your life purpose so far? Synopsize the major themes of your life experience in the section **My Life Purpose so Far.**

Reviewing all the recurring ideas and values you have discovered in your workbook exercises, fill in the section **What Matters Most to Me.**

Finally, gather together all your statements of intent, affirmations, and goals. Write them down under the section entitled **My Life Purpose Moving Forward.**

Congratulations! Take a moment to give yourself a pat on the back for your perseverance, inspiration, and willingness to move into your destiny. Not only is your life changing for the better, but you are now, most likely, in a much more insightful and hopeful place where you can be a light for others.

Shine on, Great Soul!

What I Have to Offer

_____

_____

_____

_____

_____

_____

My Current Interests

_____

_____

_____

_____

_____

_____

My Favorite Inspiring Wisdom

_____

_____

_____

_____

_____

_____

My Life Purpose So Far

_____

_____

_____

_____

_____

_____

What Matters Most to Me

_____

_____

_____

_____

_____

_____

My Life Purpose Moving Forward

_____

_____

_____

_____

_____

NOTES

CHAPTER 1: GETTING STARTED

1. Geoffrey Bownas and Anthony Thwaite (trans.), *The Penguin Book of Japanese Verse* (New York: Penguin Books, 1964), p. 71.

2. Carol Adrienne, *The Purpose of Your Life* (New York: Eagle Brook/Morrow, 1998), p. 29.

3. Margaret Wheatley and Myron Kellner Rogers, *A Simpler Way* (San Francisco: Berrett-Koehler, 1996), p. 73.

4. Adrienne, *The Purpose of Your Life*, pp. 62–63.

CHAPTER 2: INITIATION

1. Harry R. Moody, *The Five Stages of Soul: Charting the Spiritual Passages That Shape Our Lives* (New York: Anchor Books/Doubleday, 1997), p. 135.

CHAPTER 3: THE BOTTOM LINES OF MY LIFE PURPOSE—WHAT FEELS MOST IMPORTANT TO ME

1. Frances Mayes, *Under the Tuscan Sun* (New York: Broadway Books, 1996), p. 18.

2. Carol Adrienne, *The Purpose of Your Life* (New York: Eagle Brook/Morrow, 1998), p. 61.

3. Adrienne, *The Purpose of Your Life*, p. 75.

4. Adrienne, *The Purpose of Your Life*, p. 57.

5. Mayes, *Under the Tuscan Sun*, p. 178.

CHAPTER 4: MY LIFE STORY AND WHAT IT TELLS ABOUT ME

1. Carol Shields, *The Stone Diaries* (New York: Viking, 1993), p. 122.

2. Alain de Botton, *How Proust Can Change Your Life* (New York: Vintage Books, 1997), p. 13.

3. *San Francisco Chronicle*, October 24, 1998, p. A22.

4. *San Francisco Chronicle*, Nov. 24, 1998, Obituaries.

5. *San Francisco Chronicle*, February 24, 1999, p. C4 (taken from *Los Angeles Times* p. A20).

6. *San Francisco Chronicle*, Obituaries, February, 1999.

CHAPTER 5: GETTING PAST RESISTANCES

1. Quoted in Mihaly Csikszentmihalyi, *Creativity: Flow and the Psychology of Discovery and Invention* (New York: HarperCollins, 1996), p. 260.

2. Harry R. Moody, *The Five Stages of Soul: Charting the Spiritual Passages That Shape Our Lives* (New York: Anchor Books/Doubleday, 1997), p. 193.

3. Carol Adrienne, *The Purpose of Your Life* (New York: Eagle Brook/Morrow, 1998), pp. 64–65.

4. Adrienne, *The Purpose of Your Life*, p. 50.

5. Adrienne, *The Purpose of Your Life*, pp. 51–53.

CHAPTER 6: TEN COMMONLY ASKED QUESTIONS ABOUT FINDING RIGHT LIVELIHOOD

1. Jacob Needleman, *Time and the Soul* (New York: Currency/Doubleday, 1988), p. 64.

2. Needleman, *Time and the Soul*, p. 73.

3. Needleman, *Time and the Soul*, p. 117.

4. Carol Adrienne, *The Purpose of Your Life* (New York: Eagle Brook/Morrow, 1998), pp. 188–191.

5. Ralph Waldo Emerson, *Journals*, quoted in Thomas Moore, *The Education of the Heart* (New York: HarperCollins, 1997), pp. 204–205.

6. Adrienne, *The Purpose of Your Life*, p. 86.

CHAPTER 7: "BUT WHAT DO I DO?"

1. James Hillman, *The Soul's Code: In Search of Character and Calling* (New York: Random House, 1996), p. 39.

2. Willis Harman, *Global Mind Change* (San Francisco: Berrett-Koehler, 1998), p. 145.

CHAPTER 8: WRITING A WORKING PURPOSE STATEMENT

1. The Dalai Lama and Jean-Claude Carriere, *Violence and Compassion* (New York: Doubleday, 1996), pp. 120–121.

CHAPTER 9: TRACKING RELEVANT INFORMATION

1. Thomas Moore, *The Education of the Heart* (New York: HarperCollins, 1996), p. 299.

2. Nancy Rosanoff, *Intuition Workout* (Boulder Creek: Aslan Pub., 1988), p. 7.

3. Moore, *The Education of the Heart*, p. 300.

4. *San Francisco Chronicle*, October 31, 1998, p. A24.

5. Harry R. Moody, *The Five Stages of Soul: Charting the Spiritual Passages That Shape Our Lives* (New York: Anchor Books/Doubleday, 1997), p. 134.

CHAPTER 10: FUN STUFF—MAKE YOUR OWN ORACLES

1. Angeles Arrien, *Signs of Life: The Five Universal Shapes and How to Use Them* (New York: Jeremy P. Tarcher/Putnam, 1998), p. 12.

2. Angeles Arrien, *The Tarot Handbook* (Sonoma, CA: Arcus Publishing, 1987).

CHAPTER 11: DOWNLOADING AND OFFLOADING FEARS, BLOCKS, AND RESISTANCES

1. Kathleen Norris, *The Cloister Walk* (New York: Riverhead Books, 1996), p. 1.

2. George Leonard and Michael Murphy, *The Life We Are Given: A Long-Term Program for Realizing the Potential of Body, Mind, Heart, and Soul* (New York: Tarcher/Putnam, 1995), pp. 152–153.

3. Barbara Schermer, *Astrology Alive: A Guide to Experiential Astrology and the Healing Arts* (Freedom, CA: The Crossing Press, 1998), p. 230.

4. Leonard and Murphy, p. 154.

5. Leonard and Murphy, p. 155.

6. China Galland, *The Bond Between Women: A Journey of Fierce Compassion* (New York: Riverhead Books, 1998), p. 272.

7. Norris, *The Cloister Walk*, p. 165.

8. *San Francisco Chronicle*, Obituaries, December 7, 1998.

CHAPTER 12: WHERE WE LOSE POWER

1. Mark Epstein, *Thoughts Without a Thinker: Psychotherapy from a Buddhist Perspective* (New York: Basic Books, 1995), p. 19.

2. Pema Chodron, *When Things Fall Apart: Heart Advice for Difficult Times* (Boston: Shambhala Publications, 1997), p. 66.

3. Harry R. Moody, *The Five Stages of Soul: Charting the Spiritual Passages That Shape Our Lives* (New York: Anchor Books/Doubleday, 1977), p. 202.

CHAPTER 13: CREATING THE MAGIC MAGNETIC CIRCLE

1. China Galland, *The Bond Between Women: A Journey of Fierce Compassion* (New York: Riverhead Books, 1998), p. 273.

CHAPTER 14: MAKING A DIFFERENCE

1. Thom Hartmann, *The Last Hours of Ancient Sunlight: Waking Up to Personal and Global Transformation* (Northfield, VT: Mythical Books, 1998), p. 217.

2. Adapted from a news story by Kirk Semple, *San Francisco Examiner*, October 25, 1998, p. A20.

3. *The Futurist*, November/December 1996, p. 37.

4. Adapted from a news story by Jack Epstein, *San Francisco Chronicle* Foreign Service, November 2, 1998, p. A12.

5. Giorgio Cerquetti, *The Vegetarian Revolution* (Badger, CA: Torchlight Publishing, 1997), pp. 20–21.

6. Harry R. Moody, *The Five Stages of Soul: Charting the Spiritual Passages That Shape Our Lives* (New York: Anchor Books/Doubleday, 1997), p. 329.

CHAPTER 15: BEING ON PURPOSE IN THE NEW MILLENNIUM

1. Willis Harman, *Global Mind Change: The Promise of the 21st Century* (San Francisco: Berrett-Koehler, 1998), p. 100.

MASTER PROFILE OF MY LIFE PURPOSE

1. Harry R. Moody, *The Five Stages of Soul: Charting the Spiritual Passages That Shape Our Lives* (New York: Anchor Books/Doubleday, 1997), p. 335.

ABOUT THE AUTHOR

Carol Adrienne, Ph.D., an artist, numerologist, and world traveler, is also an author of spiritual growth books and an international workshop facilitator. A popular guest on radio and television, Carol appeared on *Oprah*, where the hostess lauded her book *The Purpose of Your Life: Finding Your Place in the World Using Synchronicity, Intuition, and Uncommon Sense*.

An intuitive counselor and author of books on numerology since 1976, Carol is also the coauthor with James Redfield of the *New York Times* best-seller *The Celestine Prophecy: An Experiential Guide* and *The Tenth Insight: Holding the Vision—An Experiential Guide*.

Other Life Purpose Tools by Carol Adrienne, Ph.D.

Numerology Life Chart: A 25-page personal blueprint specific to your birth name and birth date; includes interpretation of your destiny, birth path, motivation, challenges, monthly forecasts, and specific ages when major transitions occur.

    For information on how to order send:

        1) Mailing info.: name, address, day and evening phone

        2) E-mail address

Life Purpose Series of Guided Visualization Tapes:

    Tape I—Two Centering Meditations

        Side A—*For Centering Yourself and Receiving Intuitive Messages*, 24-min. meditation; increases intuition.

        Side B—*For Centering Yourself and Projecting Desires and Goals.* 26-min. meditation; focuses intention; attracts results.

    Tape II—Working Through Obstacles

        Side A *Overview*: Describes eight principles for working creatively with any problem.

        Side B *Meditation*: 40-min. in-depth guided visualization; works gently with any problem.

    Tape III—The Voices of Soul and Spirit—Two meditations with your inner feminine and masculine. Find your life vision from your feminine aspect. Manifest results with your masculine aspect.

Audio Cassettes:

        The Celestine Prophecy: An Experiential Guide

        The Tenth Insight: An Experiential Guide

        The Purpose of Your Life

Books: Available in bookstores, or order:

        The Purpose of Your Life

        The Numerology Kit—Create your own life charts. Easy how-to book with twenty-five blank charts.

        The Celestine Prophecy: An Experiential Guide: coauthored with James Redfield

        The Tenth Insight: An Experiential Guide: coauthored with James Redfield

For information about Carol's workshop calendar or to order:

The Spiral Path
6331 Fairmount Ave., Suite 422 El Cerrito, CA 94530
Tel (510) 527-2213   Fax (510) 528-2295
e-mail cadrienne@spiralpath.com   website http://www.spiralpath.com